A Guide to Getting It:

Vibrant
&
Lasting
Relationships

Jille Bartolome • Ann Golden Eglé
Patricia Eslava Vessey • Jeanie Marshall
Kathleen Oqueli McGraw • Ken Piazza Malchiodi
Marilyn Schwader • Theresa Swift
Penny R Tupy • Deb Yeagle

Marilyn Schwader, Editor

CLARITY OF VISION PUBLISHING • PORTLAND, OREGON

Other books in the series:
A Guide to Getting It: Self-Esteem
A Guide to Getting It: Achieving Abundance
A Guide to Getting It: Remarkable Management Skills
A Guide to Getting It: A Clear, Compelling Vision
A Guide to Getting It: Powerful Leadership Skills
A Guide to Getting It: Sacred Healing
A Guide to Getting It: Purpose & Passion
A Guide to Getting It: Creative Intelligence
A Guide to Getting It: Branding & Marketing Mastery

For more information, visit www.ClarityOfVision.com
To order any of the *A Guide to Getting It* book series,
visit www.ClarityOfVision.com/webstore.htm

BOOK DESIGN AND PRODUCTION BY MARILYN SCHWADER

ISBN 0-9716712-8-1
Library of Congress Control Number: 2007938025
First edition: January 2008

Table of Contents

Acknowledgments

With deep gratitude, I would like to acknowledge the wisdom, patience, and encouragement of the authors who have contributed their expertise and talents to the writing of this book. Your trust and belief through all of the obstacles and difficulties has been truly inspirational. I am blessed to have a beautiful community of colleagues, friends, and family who have provided amazing love through the ups and downs of this past year. Thank you also, to the love of my life, Margaret. Your belief in me and my work has made this book possible. I am profoundly fortunate and thankful to have such vibrant and lasting relationships in my life.

Marilyn Schwader, Editor

A Note from the Editor

The chapters in this book combine years of coaching experience with lifetimes of personal experience in the collected works of ten Life and Business Coaches. The greatest pleasure and emotional fulfillment in life is reflected through the relationships we have with each other. Whether the relationship is intimate, a friendship, within a family, or in business, this book offers ideas and techniques that are directly applicable to your own experience. Through their stories and perspectives, the authors guide you through the ins and outs, ups and downs of loving yourself and others. *Vibrant and Lasting Relationships* is an uplifting guide dedicated to bring joy and ease to every connection you make.

This unique guide will give you access to powerful, life-changing insights, examples, and exercises to help you attract, connect, and build life-long relationships.

This book is the ninth in a series of books written by Life and Business Coaches to help the reader improve their business and personal life. I invite you to read, explore, become aware, and change how you look at the relationships in your life.

Marilyn Schwader, Editor

Intentional Love:
Attracting Relationships You Truly Desire

By Marilyn Schwader

"So, what are you looking for in a relationship?" my friend asked at lunch that memorable day two years ago. The week before, I had given her the book *Ask And It is Given* by Esther and Jerry Hicks, and she wanted to talk about what she had read.

From the book and other teachings I had received in the time leading up to our conversation, I had learned to be very specific in my stated intentions, with an understanding that what you ask for is what you get, and the more precise the request, the better.

"I'd like someone who is physically attractive, intellectually stimulating, emotionally available, mentally stable, and spiritually expanding," I said with conviction and seriousness in my rote affirmation. Then I added, "But, I don't know if there's really anyone out there who has all of those attributes."

Without missing a beat, she replied, "Oh that's good, Marilyn. You just negated everything you just put out to the universe. Maybe that's why you keep having these relationships with people who aren't complete!"

After picking my jaw up from the floor, where it landed when I realized what I had been saying, I thought about exactly what it was I had been manifesting. With my belief that I wouldn't be able to find anyone with everything, I had been getting just that—relationships that fell short of the perfect match I was looking for.

Fortunately for me, I hadn't settled for any of those relationships. They had, however, brought a lot of discomfort, pain, and frustration—emotions that I didn't want to have in life. You see, the law of attraction can multiply—the more frustration I feel, the more frustration comes in to my life.

Be Careful What You Ask For

I started looking at what one of my mentors calls the "sneaky beliefs" that work against intentions (affirmations, prayers, energy—whatever name you use to describe how you ask spirit/God/universe, etc. for what you want). When I looked at other parts of my life, like finances, health, profession, family, etc., I realized that I had these little sayings, sometimes humorous, that I would add onto those intentions. For example, I'd ask for financial prosperity on the one hand, but joke to friends and family that, "Money goes out faster than it comes in!" Guess what? I didn't have a problem with the money coming in; however, it always seemed to go out faster. So, I got the prosperity, but I couldn't maintain it. You get what you ask for, even when you don't know that you are asking.

I carefully studied what I was saying in addition to my stated intention. Every time, I added something that would stop the progress dead in its tracks.

When I moved to New Mexico, I started saying, "I bring healthy, positive, and uplifting friendships into my life." What I added was, "But it's hard to find new connections in a new place."

When I had a desire to learn to still my mind, I started saying, "I claim what's meant to be in this moment." Then I added, "But, my mind just isn't cut out for meditating."

Those sneaky beliefs were everywhere I looked! Most often they appeared in "but" statements... I bring forth the perfect relationship, but I don't believe it exists... I bring forth prosperity, but it goes out faster than it comes in... I bring forth ease and joy, but life just keeps bringing in more of the opposite...

Keep in mind, those "buts" didn't always come while I was saying my affirmations. Instead, they often came up in conversations with others, in humorous things I'd say to myself, or as passing thoughts.

What I say and how I think are part of my awareness, creating that energy, no matter how slight the thought is, or how frequently I might utter a statement about that thought. When the energy is there, the law of attraction does its work, effectively canceling out the affirmation that will bring what I want into my life. Whether joking or serious, thoughts make up my belief system, even if I don't immediately realize they are a part of my thinking.

This affects all types of relationships. I have a friend who has the belief that every person that enters into her life provides a teaching that God has put in front of her to learn. If viewed from a positive perspective, with love and acceptance, this might result in expansiveness and an equal flow of energy between friends. However, she views the teaching as a burden, one that she does not want to have to face all the time. As a result, what she attracts into her life are people who don't have a tolerance for others, who are unreliable, and take more than they give. She continues to have them in her life, then wonders why her friends take so much energy. Her belief is that she has to "deal" with their idiosyncrasies because God put them in her life for a reason.

Meanwhile, her frustration at their behavior and the effect it has on her continues to build. And more reasons for frustration enter her life. It's a repeating cycle, unless she can break free from the sneaky belief that says she has to accept everyone who comes into her life. While I'm an advocate of acceptance, I don't believe that one has to promote relationships that cause harm or bring low energy vibration to your life. Everyone has choice, and if a relationship brings you down instead of lifting you up, you can choose to end that relationship in a kind, compassionate way.

Be Ready to Receive

Why then, when I removed the sneaky belief from my stated intention for a personal relationship, did it take another year before I received what I asked for? Because, although the universe always provides the answer, there is another aspect to consider: I have to be ready to receive or allow in what I am asking for.

Amazing as this might sound, the possibility of finding a partner who had all of what I thought I wanted in a relationship frightened me! All kinds of thoughts popped up. First, I looked at what I was asking for. What I realized was that I was asking for someone just like me! That alone was a scary thought. Could I live with someone else who might be like me? Would I want to? That brought up even more questions about who I viewed myself to be. Doubts arose all over the place. Would living with a reflection of myself be easy? I had a belief system that opposites attract. Finding someone like me would bash that belief system. Did I want to let it go? Was I ready to do that?

And if I did let go of that belief, would I recognize the perfect partner or would I look past them because I had never searched for that in my life and wouldn't see them if they were standing in front of me?

Oh boy, did the little thought process stir up some contradictions and doubts. And guess what? I attracted more people with contradictions and doubts. That relentless cycle hadn't been broken just yet. I still had some work to do.

So, I sat down one day with my journal and wrote down specifics of what I was looking for in another person, first, what I wanted physically: hair color, eyes, age, body type, etc. Then I wrote a detailed description of the intellectual, mental, emotional, and spiritual components.

Next, I wrote down what I liked about myself that I would want someone else to embrace. And what they might not like about me. That was an interesting exercise. I suddenly saw from as objective a viewpoint as I could about myself, what I needed to change in order to be in a relationship.

Without realizing it, I was creating a new container with new beliefs about myself and, ultimately, what I could attract into my life. Until I made that container solid and whole, I wouldn't be able to receive what the universe wanted to provide. In that moment, I decided to do some fixing of myself before I looked any further.

I took that list and began. First, I wanted to be healthy— physically, mentally, and emotionally. If I wanted that from someone else, I had to walk the talk. I changed my diet, started a new exercise routine, and began to release ideas of myself that I didn't like. This was not an overnight process; it took months. However, as each day passed, I saw progress.

My mentor suggested that I repeat a specific mantra 500 times per day. At first I resisted. Five hundred times a day! I couldn't do that—or so I thought. Slowly, I lowered my resistance, starting with 100. Remarkably, I started to feel so good with 100 per day that I wondered what it would feel like saying it 200 times. In a short time, I reached 500 per day, and soon, everything in my world started to change. What I was saying was in complete alignment with the law of attraction, and my external world was reflecting how much better I felt inside and out.

I felt very good about my intellectual pursuits, and welcomed a relationship with that component. The remaining aspect was the spiritual component. When I realized that all of the other work I was doing on me was tied to my spiritual growth, I accepted that this would be an ever-expanding part of my life. I embraced its place in my work, my communication, my family, and my friendships.

At that point, I felt my container was ready to allow in an intimate relationship. I was ready to welcome in what I had been asking for in the months and years of being alone.

Then I had a setback. I had traveled to Scotland to present a writing retreat, then spent a week visiting an acquaintance in Belgium and seeing the sights in western Europe. I had a lovely time, with many significant memories. I had decided that after I returned from that holiday, I would start dating again.

In the middle of the night before I was to fly home, I awoke with severe stomach pains. Having had food poisoning on two prior occasions, I knew immediately that I had it again... and I wouldn't be flying home that day.

Because my flight was so early in the morning, the recording on the airline's voice message instructed me to go to the airport to change flights. My friend drove me there, dropped me off at the terminal, then went to park the car. By the time she arrived to see what had transpired, I had collapsed, hitting the floor face first, and not able to move. I was taken to the hospital, given fluids, and told to rest.

On returning to the airport to retrieve my friend's car, I collapsed again, this time on the concrete pavement, smashing face first into the ground. I sustained a severe concussion, a nearly broken nose, and my teeth had pierced through my upper lip. I was a bloody mess.

Two days later, I finally arrived home. That night, bandaged face and all, I went to a friend's birthday party, despite having jet lag and low energy from what I now call the Belgium Bashing. All the work I had done to create a new me was a distant thought. I was clearly not myself to those who knew me. That night, I apparently met a woman named Margaret, but if you had asked me the next day, I would not have been able to tell you who she was.

A week later, I attended a fund-raiser dance for a friend who had lost a leg in a boating accident. Still banged up, but wanting to begin dating again, I had strategically applied the Band-aids and makeup to cover up the remaining wounds. While there, a woman approached me, introduced herself as "Margaret", and said our mutual friend, Carla, had suggested we have coffee. I was focused on another woman that I wanted to ask for a date, so I suggested to Margaret that she go ask Carla why she thought we should get to know each other. Margaret dutifully left to ask her the question. I refocused my attention on the other woman.

Margaret was soon making her way across the room toward me again. She was tall, with red hair, confident, and a moved with the grace of an athlete. Having always dated shorter, darker women (like the woman I was pursuing), there was no connection for me. Once again I rebuffed her attempt at conversation. A few minutes later, she returned, handed me her phone number, and said, "Look, I'm not asking you for a date. I just want to find out why Carla thinks I should get to know you." Then she walked away.

I still wasn't interested in dating her, but I was intrigued. I liked her directness. "Maybe Carla's right. She might be a good friend," I thought to myself. I pocketed her number and a few days later called to arrange a time to meet for coffee. Our schedules never worked out and eventually we both gave up.

Nearly two months later, I saw her and Carla at a dance. After having danced with several other friends, I asked if she wanted a turn on the dance floor. She reluctantly said yes. As we danced, the connection that had been missing, that energy that says, "Hmmmmm. I like how that feels" clicked. We finished the dance, and as the next song started, a friend grabbed me to dance. I looked over my shoulder to see where Margaret was, and saw a mixture of confusion, surprise, and happiness on her face. She was standing on the edge of the room watching me. "I think I want to ask her out," I thought to myself. "And I'll bet she does, too." She and Carla left a short time later. I called her the next day.

Two weeks later, we went out on a date. A year has passed and we are making plans for a life together.

She told me that she barely remembered meeting me at the birthday party, and swears I had no bandages on my face at the fundraiser. In fact, what she remembers is that I didn't have any energy—no pizzazz, no reason for her to want to get to know me. And she was right. The Belgium Bashing had been a deflating experience and I was recovering from a concussion. My normal, high-frequency vibration of energy was missing. She wasn't attracted to me. She was interested in being with someone who had a more vibrant energy. That was a huge example to me of the power of the law of attraction in action.

What we know now is that we are perfectly matched. We have the same values, the same outlook on life. The importance of family is primary for both of us. We love animals and dancing. We look for joy in life. We are spiritually expanding in phenomenal ways. We even look like sisters, as friends and strangers often remind us.

Yes, there are differences, but they are few and not significant. The universe has given me what I was asking for: a complete person who compliments my life, and me hers. We asked, and it was given.

Manifesting the Relationship You Want

You, too, can manifest the relationships you want in your life; and you can let go of those that don't work. You have the ability and the choice to do that. First, you must identify what it is that you are truly asking for, and what you believe. Then examine if you are truly ready for what it is you are asking. And yes, it takes work to change beliefs that have been entrenched for years.

The question to ask yourself is if what you want is worth the effort it will take to change? If it is, then you will find the answers. Because, you see, the desire to have it creates the energy to make it so. What will be different for everyone is how quickly the change is made that is necessary to bring that intention into your life.

Start by examining yourself. Write down what you see and what you want to change. Write down what you want in a relationship, whether it's a friendship or an intimate partner. Then write down how you will begin to make the change necessary for you to accept it in your life. Finally, write down when you would like to receive it. Make the time for this exercise, and you will soon be on your way to manifesting what you want.

And each time you feel you have made progress, stop for a moment and give thanks for what you are bringing into your life. Because the highest frequency vibration there is, is gratitude. The more thankful you are for the blessings in your life, the more blessings will flow to you. It's the law of attraction in action. Do these simple steps, and for the rest of your life, you will experience a vibrant and lasting relationship with yourself and all of the people you truly want in your life.

About
Marilyn Schwader

As a Writing and Life Coach, Marilyn Schwader uses humor, compassion, and a strong sense of a writer's abilities to support and motivate her clients to become published authors. She has found that her purpose in life is to give a voice to subjects that benefit others. Her mission is to provide truthful, clear, and motivating information to those who passionately desire more in their lives. Her vision is to use her two passions—coaching and storytelling—to convey this information to as many people as possible.

Marilyn graduated from Oregon State University in Corvallis, Oregon with a Bachelor of Science degree in Technical Journalism with emphasis in Business Management. After working for several years as a technical writer contracting to high tech companies in the United States and Pacific Rim countries, she veered from the writing path and started her first business, M's Tea & Coffee House, in Corvallis.

Five years and numerous disastrous business mistakes later, she left the restaurant business and a short time later discovered Coaching. In 1998 she enrolled in Coach University and started Clarity of Vision, Inc., a Business and Life Coaching practice. The law of attraction soon worked its magic, and her talents and experience in writing soon began drawing writing clients to her business.

During this time, Marilyn undertook a three-year project to compile and publish a book about her mother's family history. From that experience, she began helping people self-publish their books. Looking for a way to combine her coaching and writing experience, Marilyn decided to create a book series that would be written by coaches and that highlighted principles and ideas supported in the coaching process.

Thus, the *A Guide to Getting It* book series was born. *A Guide to Getting It: Vibrant & Lasting Relationships* is the ninth book in the series. The first eight books are:

A Guide to Getting It: Self-Esteem

A Guide to Getting It: Achieving Abundance

A Guide to Getting It: Remarkable Management Skills

A Guide to Getting It: A Clear, Compelling Vision

A Guide to Getting It: Powerful Leadership Skills

A Guide to Getting It: Sacred Healing

A Guide to Getting It: Purpose & Passion

A Guide to Getting It: Creative Intelligence

Visit www.ClarityOfVision.com to find out more about the *Guide to Getting It* book series, classes Marilyn is teaching, and for information about how to write, publish, and promote your knowledge products. To contact Marilyn, call 503-460-0014 or email Marilyn@ClarityOfVision.com

Falling In Love...
With Yourself

By Ann Golden Eglé

"The unexamined life is not worth living." ~ Socrates

For such a bright guy, Phillip seemed lost. His friends were concerned that he never fully committed himself to any one person or thing, diving in with both feet, fully energized about each new endeavor, and then becoming disinterested just as quickly, before the candle was fully lit. The master of shedding any hint of responsibility, someone else was always at fault. Though on paper he seemed to have it all—wife, kids, job, and home—Phillip was not happy. He was one big walking lie, even to himself.

Phillip's home life spoke volumes about whom he had become. His family stayed far away from him after his arrival from work each day, fearing that they would once again hear every rotten thing that occurred during his day, along with who was to blame. He never shared the good stuff with them; perhaps there was no good stuff. Sadly, Phillip also missed the grand events occurring in his own household, like Kelly making the soccer team and Cody's last report card.

How did it come to this? Phillip was a popular child and adolescent. He attained good grades and teachers liked him. When and where did things take a turn from his being a welcome part of the party to people scattering when he entered the room? To answer those questions, it was first important to ask two vital questions that I ask all of my executive coaching clients:

What's it like to be inside Phillip's head?
How does he see and interpret the world around him?

Three words soon came to light—victim, lost, and manipulation. He was in fact lost. Phillip had a gaping hole in his heart that he attempted to fill with blame, negativity, manipulation, and avoidance. When I asked him about this gaping hole he was first in denial, and then claimed it too difficult to go there. To no surprise, he wanted to manipulate our focus.

His parents did this, siblings did that, teachers and friends were all to blame for some faction of his inner misery. Phillip took no responsibility, but could place plenty on everyone else in his world. He considered himself "... just fine. Everyone else needs fixing."

Though his manipulation started as a child, it was not evident until his professional years, when Phillip refused to take responsibility for, well, anything. As a child and adolescent he was not expected to take responsibility and thus could skate by with jokes, finger pointing, and steering clear of anything relevant to discovering his true worth.

We discovered precisely what Phillip was missing—himself! Victims and manipulators rarely have any idea of who they are on the inside. They have an extraordinary fear of self-discovery as they may not like what they find. In contrast, a common factor in the type of individual who seeks a professional coach is that they see a gap between where they are and where they want to be. Phillip was not this self aware, not even close. Why had he engaged my services then? Because his CEO saw the gap, yet also saw tremendous value in Phillip and wanted to see him overcome his inner obstacles.

To draw Phillip away from his focus on outer activities and events was indeed a challenge. He truly had no idea who he was or what made him happy. He admitted to receiving fractured hints from how others treated and reacted to him, but he had no clear picture of who he was in his heart. Phillip was able to do a marginal job at work and at home, but there was so much more he could experience in life if he simply had a stronger self knowledge, if he could only look inside to see the mastery and wisdom and stop blaming or manipulating others.

Taking time to know ourselves is awkward at first, just like getting to know another person, yet it is perhaps the most worthwhile endeavor that we'll undertake on this earth.

It's far easier to come up with excuses: "Getting to know myself? Isn't that selfish? I don't have time and it just plain sounds like nonsense. Isn't that some New Age garble?"

Phillip begrudgingly agreed that he had nothing to lose by taking on this new venture. It is one thing to say that having a relationship with yourself is a pretty good idea with benefits beyond your current understanding, but quite another to know where to start. To many of us it just sounds too big—like years and years of writing in your journal and going to therapy. The key is baby steps.

Phillip's experience demonstrated that it can happen much more easily and quickly with the proven tools and techniques I'll introduce to you below. (You'll find a summary of these tools at the end of this chapter.) I invite you to take this journey with Phillip.

My request of Phillip as we went through these stages is the same that I now make of you: Go into it as a student. Be willing to try anything in the name of learning. If you are willing to get to know yourself better, why not go all the way and fall in love with the magnificent person you are? This was understandably a tough concept for Phillip, and perhaps it is for you. Remember, be a wide-eyed, open student.

Falling in love with "you" is no different than falling in love with another person. The challenge is that we've grown up with models of actors and relatives loving others while we were given harsh words warning against paying too much attention to who we are at the core. We were warned constantly against tooting our own horn, getting too big of a head, being too boastful. Thus, to ease the challenge of getting to know the real Phillip, we compared each step to falling in love with another.

First, you notice that the other person exists and something tells you that that there is value in getting to know him or her. Then, infatuation sets in. This is followed by immense curiosity, creative ideas about how and when you can spend time together, excitement, more intense focus, and moments of doubt and fear, requiring commitment of time and hours of communication. It's as if you cannot get enough of this other person. Time flies by, spirits are elevated, life is grand. You're in the flow, and not much else matters.

Let's break this down into simple components along with how Phillip experienced and learned from each. Know that this is a process, not an afternoon exercise. If you take this journey, please allow time to go through each step slowly. One must not rush falling in love.

Attraction (Infatuation)

"Do you love me because I'm beautiful?
Or am I beautiful because you love me?"
~ Oscar Hammerstein, II

Seemingly out of nowhere someone captures your attention through being distinctive—the way they walk, talk, the sparkle in their eyes, their intelligence, vulnerability, humor, beauty, or smile. You are intrigued, feel a little giddy, and ask yourself, "Just what is it about this person that has moved me?" All of the sudden time stands still and you begin to notice every nuance.

Everything is important, from the tone of their voice, to what makes them laugh, to the essence of their stories. What are they really sharing with you? Are they allowing you into their inner world and, if so, just what makes this such a fascinating place to be? You have to remind yourself to breathe as you focus on this individual.

Now switch the focus to you. Stand back and observe yourself with the same amount of fascination. What is unique about you? Look in the mirror. What happens when you smile, look intrigued, sad, excited, and enthused? What is the mirror reflecting back?

If you've not allowed yourself to stare deeply in the mirror for such feedback in the past, please be prepared. Most people look for things they don't like when looking in the mirror, like that bulging belly or laugh wrinkles around the eyes and mouth. Allow a few moments to get beyond those factors. Just breathe and let them go, as they have no bearing at this moment. When getting to know someone who intrigues you, it's easy to either overlook such factors, or to see them as intriguing clues into their character.

Look deep into your eyes. What are they telling you? What is there to know about this fascinating person looking back? Now look at your posture. Sit, stand, talk, listen, and interact with this person looking back. Who is this person? Is he perhaps funnier than you thought? Is she more confident, shy, stunning, or brilliant? What questions do you have? Let them flow and jot them down. This is an ongoing exercise, not merely one to do today and it's over. Allow your learning to continue each time you look in the mirror. Breathe and take time to enjoy this process; after all it is your process.

Now look...

For Phillip, to start with the mirror work was just too difficult. This was no surprise as his focus was outside. So, that's where we started — outside of himself. He began his inner process by writing down what people reflected back to him in the way of feedback. What did they value in him? This is no time to be timid or shy. With practice he became more bold, honest, and thorough than ever before.

He discovered that it was necessary to write down the negatives that bombarded his mental process in order to release them to focus on the positive aspects that people reflected back to him. Phillip wrote those on a separate sheet, as they weren't relevant at this point. When you first get to know someone who captivates you, you are only interested in what is fascinating about them. After a short period, Phillip did in fact move on to the mirror work as his curiosity was energized. Would he see the same person that others saw in him? His questions began to flow.

Now you're on your way. You've noticed yourself, written down some questions, and perhaps observations. You are intrigued enough to go to that next step of falling in love.

The First Date (Curiosity)

"LIFE IS MEANT TO BE LIVED. CURIOSITY MUST BE KEPT ALIVE."
~ ELEANOR ROOSEVELT

It's time to gratify your curiosity. You've seen some surface and below-surface uniqueness about yourself, decided that there is more than meets the eye, and are now eager to learn more.

How does one go about that with another person? Set aside your nagging self-criticism, and plan your first date.

This gets a little tricky, but if you are reading this chapter, I know you are up to it. Here, you will be both the pursuer (observer) and the object of your affection (one being pursued). Have fun with both roles, as both will provide a unique insight to who you are.

Where shall we go on this first date? If there is anything you'd like to do this evening or weekend, what would it be? No judgment, just listen to your heart and jot ideas down as they flow to you.

What will provide you the greatest insight into who you are? What locations or activities will create an atmosphere of bliss? What insights will this provide? For years, Phillip never took time to ask himself what he wanted. Instead, he gave his power to anyone who came along. It's time for you to claim your power and say what you want.

Will it be a museum to go back in history, a tree house to get back to nature, skydiving to see life from an eagle's vantage point? How about a fine arts exhibit, rock concert, walk on the beach, breakfast in Rome, or lunch in Paris? Dream at a level that stretches you. Close your eyes and imagine yourself in this place, eagerly asking and answering questions the way two lovers do when first uniting.

Next, write down 100 questions you'd ask another person on a first date. Do this quickly and intuitively, not worrying about the answers for now. They can be things ranging from curiosity about the date to what their grandmother and grandfather's relationship was like. Be wild and let it flow. There is no right or wrong. What do you want to know? Sometimes a question is the best way to make a statement. What do you want to share with this magnificent person who makes your heart throb?

Phillip's first date was to Moab, bicycling with a childhood buddy whom he could trust to provide honest feedback and insight. By being away from it all, his questions flowed. He could hardly write fast enough to capture all of the directions that his curiosity took him. Initial questions led to more questions and the process continued with blinding speed.

Second Date (Dreams Unveiled)

"There is nothing like a dream to create the future."
~ Victor Hugo

So how was your first date? Now that you've gone beyond some of the awkward stages of any first date, are you willing to continue the process of getting to know yourself? That's what second dates are all about. But before you go on your second date, take time to process the first date in whatever method works for you—journaling, walking, running, talking with a friend. Allow yourself to get giddy. You're getting to know a whole new person in your world—you.

No matter how well you know yourself, these exercises will take you to a whole new level. The process has just begun, so be patient. What discoveries have you made to date? Is this enjoyable, intriguing, challenging? Are you uncovering dreams that have been long forgotten?

Write or talk about where you went on your first date. What did you learn? How vivid was it? Was there laughter or tears? Intimacy? Surprises? Did you unveil secrets that were previously too private to share, or that had not previously even been known to you? How was it to have someone listen to you so intently? Are you ready for more?

On this second date, you'll continue to tackle more of those 100 questions you asked on your first date. Again, do this quickly and intuitively. No need for perfection here. You are merely getting to know what's important to you here and now. You are not competing in a spelling bee or on *Jeopardy*. There is simply no judgment, just fascination with this individual whom you're getting to know.

You may experience a shift in answering the questions. Some of what you thought was important yesterday may not be today, and vice versa. The focus is on who you are at this very moment. The past is in the past. Did it help to mold you? Is it a part of your character today? Perhaps, but not necessarily. Sometimes, it molded you into the opposite of what occurred. For example, a bullied teen may turn into a compassionate, supportive parent because of his experiences. What is important is that you look at what and who you are at this very moment. What do you believe in? What do you stand for? What is your essence?

Allow these answers to gently stream out in whatever direction feels right for the setting. Breathe; be gentle and patient with yourself. You can't force the answers any more than you would force a second date to answer. Nor would you harshly judge. Some answers may lead to more questions. Allow your unique process to unfold as it will. You have time. And this time is so very well spent.

To Phillip's utter surprise, the answers flowed quickly and easily. It was as though he had this other being inside of him who had been silenced for years. This person, his true essence, now had permission to speak, and that he did—sharing as one does when first opening up to a nonjudgmental person with whom they feel safe. The insight that was immediate and abundant would have been impossible for Phillip to access in any other manner. He was now fully engaged in this process and ready for more.

Third Date (Create Time)

"COME OUT OF THE CIRCLE OF TIME AND INTO THE CIRCLE OF LOVE."
~RUMI

Time flew by on your first two dates, partially fueled by excitement. As your third date approaches, issues of time leak in. If you think that you don't have time to devote to this process, you are dead wrong. If something happened to a family member today, you'd find time. If the person of your dreams walked into your life today, you'd find time. If someone handed you $5 million to contribute to the charity of your choice and it was only available with your direct participation, you'd create the time. Now it's your spirit who's calling to you to make time to listen and act.

What creative ideas are available to you for carving out time for yourself each day? Yes, I said each and every day! No relationship thrives without time and attention. Take time to observe yourself not only as you are today, but as you evolve through each stage of life from this day forward.

You've heard of typical ways to find more time for yourself, such as wake up early, stay up after the kids are in bed, take lunch hours alone, or drive in silence. While all of these will work beautifully, there are other ideas that are uniquely available to you. Shhh, close your eyes and think of how you can devote luscious, quality time to yourself.

Phillip discovered that even a few minutes several times each day worked profoundly for him. He would close his door, turn away from the computer, close his eyes, and focus on his breathing. Weather permitting, he would schedule lunch meetings close to his office, allowing him to walk, enjoying the sights and sounds of nature along the way. He also discovered various locations within and outside his building where he could relax periodically. To his amazement, he discovered the art of people-watching, not to manipulate or change them, but simply to observe as though each one had something to teach him.

The benefits he reaped from crafting moments in time for himself far outweighed the challenges. As an added value in his more creative approach to time, he found more time to value those important to him. Creating time for this third date was indeed a win/win scenario.

Fourth, Fifth, Sixth Dates (Cherish the Excitement)

"SOMETIMES YOUR JOY IS THE SOURCE OF YOUR SMILE, BUT SOMETIMES YOUR SMILE CAN BE THE SOURCE OF YOUR JOY." ~ THICH NHAT HANH

Ah, getting to know you, getting to know all about you—truly, isn't the process intriguing? It's worth your precious time. You've looked into the mirror, asked and answered some revealing questions, and perhaps surprised yourself along the way. The next few dates are intended to allow you to settle into the excitement of this recent unveiling and deepen your learning.

Relax. Allow the excitement to illuminate you. Each new date brings new discoveries. Continue to allow creativity to flow with your dates. Take yourself to the park, a movie, a restaurant you've only read about. Enjoy and cherish this rich process.

In discovering more about "who" and "why" you are, you may also find yourself increasing your gratitude—to whatever creator you believe in, to those around you who serve as your teachers, to those who generously love you. In allowing your bliss, you let go of parts of you that no longer serve you. You see yourself in a new light.

Phillip released unhealthy assumptions, along with the need to blame others for the results he created in his life. In catching himself wanting to manipulate others, he simply stopped, checked in with himself, and asked himself: "Is this what you really want?" The answers were much clearer with each encounter. He was no longer lost or a victim.

Perhaps you can see that glow. I have no doubt that others are witness to it, though they are not aware of what is changing inside you. You may hear from them: "Have you lost weight, cut your hair, changed from glasses to contacts?" Perhaps you have, but that isn't the real glow they notice. It comes from within you because you are now creating a relationship with yourself, one that will forever alter the way you see yourself and how you allow others to see you.

As you flow through this process, continue to ask yourself just what is unique to you and you alone? Science shows that there is no one quite like you on the planet. Sure, others can run, but do you run for a cause? Others can speak, but is yours a unique message that will change lives? What is it that you want to be, do, accomplish during your lifetime? Begin to envision this very thing, not the "how-to" but the finish line. The rest will come in time.

There is only one magnificent you. Look again in the mirror at those amazing eyes and get excited about what's next for you now that you are realizing and accepting your gifts.

Seventh Date (Quiet the Voice of Doubt)

"CREATIVITY REQUIRES THE COURAGE TO LET GO OF CERTAINTIES."
~ ERICH FROMM

With every new venture comes an element of uncertainty. Our critical voice boldly enters making judgments, reeking havoc with our confidence. "What are you doing? Who do you think you are?" This doubt appears when we are not fully in our game, when we are overworked, tired, out of balance, or sick. Things seem out of whack. Phillip lived his life in this mode for years, never questioning and instead believing the lies of his damaging, critical inner voice.

By its very nature, the dating process is ripe for doubt and fear. You are accessing parts of who you are that have previously been available only to those who love you and perhaps not even to them. You are completely vulnerable.

If you have done the exercises and are committed to this process, you may be on a high with your self-discovery. That high cannot last forever.

As with breathing in and breathing out, there is a flow with your emotions. It's up to you to make sure that flow is consistent and your high does not also result in the other end of the pendulum—the lowest of lows. Uncertainty is a natural that keeps us on our toes. Just don't confuse it with sadness or depression. Our emotions require attention, understanding, and balance.

Easier said than done? Living a balanced life helps quiet the voice of doubt. This means that you live life "in your game". Being in your game means getting back to your basics. This is as true for business as it is for you as an individual. A business runs in to trouble when it stretches too much beyond what made it profitable in the first place, like customer service or a high quality product. These are their basics. Basics create balance, strength, and success in any endeavor. What basics will keep you on top of your game?

Phillip learned that his basics are not negotiable. Without exercise, eating right, proper sleep, hydration, focus on relationships (including with himself), tuning into his core values, and creating alone or pensive time each day, he is simply out of whack. When he is out of whack, the voice of fear and doubt bombards his thoughts and he quickly reverts to past behaviors of blame and manipulation. Clearly, these are not relationship builders on the seventh or any date. These behaviors are an instant red flag for him to get back to his basics.

Know when it is time to get back to your basics. No one can do this for you. It's all up to you to first know what your basics are and then to create a lifestyle that honors each one.

Eighth Date (Build Trust)

"TRUST THYSELF: EVERY HEART VIBRATES TO THAT IRON STING.
SELF TRUST IS THE FIRST SECRET TO SUCCESS."
~ RALPH WALDO EMERSON

By the eighth date, you realize that there is more to you than meets the eye. You are in fact beginning to fall in love with yourself—foibles and all. A vital part of falling in love is establishing a true sense of trust. How do you create trust within yourself? What are the components of trust?

First, there is consistency of behavior. You feel trust in a person when you know how they will consistently treat, respect, and protect you. If your self talk is damaging, you have no more trust than you would with a friend who consistently belittled you. Part of this phase is to pay very close attention to the workings of your inner mind.

We pay little attention to our own self talk or how damaging our daily messages can be. For example, after a meeting do you say, "You idiot, why didn't you speak up?" Or, are you more respectful with, "This is a safe group with whom I can be myself and show my true colors. I needn't impress anyone; instead, I intend to be a stronger part of the team. Next time I'll come more prepared."

Second, there is consistency of time. You've undoubtedly noted that committing time is a common trait in falling in love. Establish a consistent time to devote to yourself each week, preferably each day. Make it a priority. It's hard to fall in love with someone who is on the bottom of your list. Another benefit is the law of attraction. If you put yourself on the top of your list, you'll attract others who treat you in a similar manner.

Third, there is consistency of attitude. When we fall in love, everything, literally everything, in our world is lighter, more clear and easier. Is it that the outer world changes to honor our current state of mind? Quite the opposite, as we are responsible to create an amazing outer world through our intentional actions, thoughts, and attitude.

As you grow more in love with yourself, your gifts, and what brings you true happiness, you'll be hard-pressed not to have a consistent attitude that will allow the world to reflect this back to you.

Establishing trust was a difficult, albeit huge growth experience for Phillip. He began to further question his assumptions, identifying old habits of avoiding responsibility. For him to truly trust himself meant accepting full responsibility for everything that he created in his inner and outer world. He could no longer blame others for not attaining the results he desired. In time, Phillip not only gained greater trust for himself, but for those around him and them for him. This was a life-changing phase indeed.

Final Stages of Falling in Love (Commitment)

"LOVE DOESN'T MAKE THE WORLD GO 'ROUND;
LOVE IS WHAT MAKES THE RIDE WORTHWHILE."
~ FRANKLIN P. JONES

The time has come to ask if it's worth it. You've done the initial exercises, explored who you are in many new and exciting venues. You've looked at yourself in a brand new light. Is it worth making a commitment to this lifelong process of further discovering who and what you are?

If you say, "Absolutely," then you're ready for the final phase: Commit to yourself. Commit to repeating these exercises as often as your intuition suggests. Know that each time you repeat an exercise will look different depending on your frame of mind. Such repetition will take you to deeper and deeper levels of self-discovery, self love. You are not the same person you were one year ago, nor are you the same person who you'll be one year from today. There is still so much to learn.

When we look at ourselves through eyes of love we see how much is possible, not what is impossible. We see growth and opportunity, where our true beauty can shine. We easily eliminate what is not working for us in order to make more room for what honors us in the life we are creating.

As you continue the habit of looking deep into the artwork of your eyes, for example, continue to allow your curiosity to flow. Continue to ask and answer questions from your heart.

Or, be silent and take in your abundance, exquisiteness, strength, and wisdom. What have these eyes seen? What has brought tears? Laughter? Enthusiasm? Sadness? Get lost in the depth of your eyes as you would in the eyes of a new lover. Your eyes have much to say to you. Be silent as your gaze takes you beyond what is comfortable.

Continue to ask specific questions and see what comes back. Again, this is a process of allowing data to come to you, never forcing. You are on no timeline. With practice, you'll be pleasantly surprised at how much your eyes and heart have to say to you.

As for Phillip, he did end up on top of his game. The gaping hole in his heart is being filled a little more each day. Through working on the above exercises over time, Phillip learned just how impossible it is to strengthen any relationship (including one with himself) without curiosity, vulnerability, time, focus, communication, trust, and commitment.

For years, Phillip's eyes mirrored sadness to him, sadness that he'd not allowed them to be seen or his heart to be heard. Today, it is a completely different story—a love story, in fact.

Though the concept of "loving himself" sounded preposterous to Phillip when we first met, he was willing to go the distance in order to create a life other than what he had created. To the sheer delight of his wife, children, friends, CEO, and associates, Phillip now enjoys life and is a welcome participant in any scenario. Those around him are now eager to hear what he has to share.

He walks with a new sense of eagerness to go out and experience everything in this world because he has a strong foundation, the foundation that only self love can provide.

I challenge you to make these exercises a lifelong commitment from you to you. This is an evolutionary process. Anais Nin states: "Love never dies a natural death. It dies because we don't know how to replenish its source." Your ability to love and understand yourself will be multiplied with your continual focus, attention, and dedication.

I would love to hear how this process is for you!

Summary of Tools and Techniques for Each Stage

Attraction (Infatuation): Notice what's unique about you; mirror work; ask initial questions; list feedback with arrows to true meaning.

1st Date (Curiosity): Where would you go; list 100 intriguing questions.

2nd Date (Dreams Unveiled): Begin to intuitively answer your 100 questions; notice the shift in what is important to you today; let go of the rest.

3rd Date (Create Time): Create time to devote to the process of falling in love with you.

4th, 5th & 6th Dates (Cherish the Excitement): What are you learning? Relish in the excitement of what you are learning; continue to realize just how unique you are; listen to what others are noticing about you.

7th Date (Quiet the Doubt): Get back to your basics and in your game.

8th Date (Build Trust): Be consistent in self talk, time, and attitude.

Falling in Love (Commitment): Make it real. Commit to yourself. Continue the process of looking into your eyes, being curious, and deepening your learning through journaling, running, silence, or discussion.

About
Ann Golden Eglé

Master Certified Coach Ann Golden Eglé (pronounced egg-lay) took the long route to having a relationship with herself. Growing up the middle kid in the family in the middle of the USA, she learned to become invisible at an early age.

In all of her professional endeavors, Eglé reached the highest level of success, from being a teen model to excelling in fashion merchandising, sales and marketing, economic development planning and serving as the President of a Visitor and Convention Bureau, and top 1% nationally-ranked Realtor. With all of these achievements there was always something missing.

Eglé's world turned around when she hired an executive coach in 1996. She soon learned that her previous motto of: "I am my own worst enemy" no longer represented who she was, not that it ever really did. Eglé's motto is now: "It's simply not difficult to become highly successful. The key is to not lose yourself in the process."

Fascinated with the clarity that executive coaching had brought to her life, Eglé spent a year studying and was awarded certification to practice through The Coaches Training Institute. Golden Visions Success Coaching, LLC, was established in 1998 and remains one of the most successful Executive Success Coaching practices in the country. Eglé has published over 25 articles on Success, Executive Development, and Leadership. Her free weekly *Success Tip* e-zine is distributed to recipients in ten countries (subscribe on her web site).

Eglé's niche since day one has been highly successful individuals. This is based on three theories: 1) there is a lot of help for those climbing the ladder, but little for those who've reached the top. They know that it truly can be a lonely place with few, if any, individuals with whom to confide, explore ideas, be authentic, and vulnerable; 2) We are all great at that one thing that carries us to the top, yet few of us have the necessary skill sets to be highly effective overall once we get there; 3) As one becomes more successful, the need for balance to maintain that high level of mental and emotional activity becomes even greater. Finding a workable professional/personal balance is difficult enough, and when you throw in an element of time for oneself, it often becomes unattainable.

Eglé helps her highly successful clients in such areas as effective communication, compassion, getting out of their own way, self-talk, damaging assumptions, being a better listener and being more decisive, and seeing the larger picture—an array of personal issues that go hand-in-hand with success.

Eglé was awarded the prestigious designations of Master Certified Coach (MCC) in 2005 and Advanced Toastmaster Bronze in 2002. Additionally, she was named one of the top "Women in Business" by the Cascade Business News in 2007 for her contributions to both business and the community.

She resides on the Stargazer Ranch in Oregon with her husband and an assortment of beloved four-legged family members. Ann welcomes your comments at www.GVSuccess.com, ann@gvsuccess.com, or 541-385-8887.

Discovering Your Core Heart Essence: CHE™

By Patricia Eslava Vessey

Her palms were moist and her mouth was dry. As she stood at the edge of the stage, she took a deep breath in, and with it, she allowed feelings about the past year to fill every cell of her body. "I feel so good," she thought with joy in her heart, and as she exhaled, she felt the tension in her body completely dissolve. She knew that her speech to these 500 people at the Institute could change their lives forever, and she was eager to start.

She began: "Let me tell you about someone I once knew..."

Anna was a highly successful CEO in charge of a service that helps people abused and disadvantaged by life's worst tragedies. Through her influential reputation, Anna gained national recognition and numerous leadership awards for outstanding performance and dedication. Many disadvantaged people were helped by her extraordinary efforts. Work was her life, and she poured every ounce of herself into doing an extraordinary job at everything she did.

In her late 50's, never married, and with few "real" friends, Anna completely lost herself in her work. Some say it was her only passion. When she wasn't working at the company office, she worked at her home office. She felt most alive immersing herself in the busyness of her job. She often made business calls late in the evening, and worked until the early hours of the morning.

In return, Anna felt important, needed, and most of all, she felt she had a purpose. In addition, her work provided an ulterior benefit—pouring herself into her job kept her from facing her fear of being close to people, a deep-rooted insecurity that was only outdone by her fear of being close to herself. Anna held a great deal of pain, disappointment, and heartache in her body, and working was a buffer and distraction. When she worked, she didn't have to feel and think about anything else.

She didn't know much about herself, her personal values, or who she was at her core. What she did know well, was how to play the successful, powerful, and influential role as CEO. Anna refused to think about what was truly important to her. It was too painful and unproductive to allow herself to think about what she didn't have. When these thoughts emerged, she quickly dismissed them. Instead, she focused on her "to do" list, checking off and adding to the numerous and important work-related tasks.

Stepping outside her work role, Anna floundered like a fish out of water. She purposely avoided office parties and social gatherings because she felt uncomfortable mingling and talking about anything other than work.

Anna's secret fear was that people would discover she wasn't as good at her job as they believed; that they would think she was a fraud, not good enough for the high level position she held. Sometimes she would lie awake all night, imagining terrifying scenes about failing at her job, and she'd be filled with dread and panic, sure that she was losing something very important.

On rare occasions, Anna remembered when she used to paint and the passionate connection she felt while doing it. She was a brilliant and gifted artist who at one time thought of opening an art gallery. But, she convinced herself that work was more important than her own interests. Instead of appreciating and honoring this passion, she set it aside. If she just kept busy enough, she wouldn't have to think about what she was missing.

Anna's family immigrated to America when she was a small child. Growing up in the slums of New York, kids in her neighborhood teased and tormented her for the poverty she lived in, for her accent, and her family customs. She grew up feeling inadequate, and turned to the business world for success, dedicating her life to being the best, and in this, she found her worth.

Two failed relationships in her 20's created lifelong scars. Anna was terrified of intimacy, although she secretly longed for marriage and children. Instead, she married her job, living with it day and night. There was no boundary between personal life and work life. They were one and the same. She worked to live and lived to work. Inside and out, Anna became successful at disconnecting with her inner self.

With her relentless focus on work, Anna's health problems had progressively worsened over the years. Her job completely consumed her life. Anna could never seem to find time to care for herself by exercising, eating healthy food, taking vacations, spending time with friends, or seeing doctors on a regular basis. "I am too busy at work to go to the gym or even go on vacation," she told colleagues. She used this excuse repeatedly, and everyone accepted it. After all, it was a noble thing to cast your self aside in sacrifice to help the less fortunate. Soon, they stopped asking if she was taking a vacation.

Always making herself available to take on extra work, her company continued to add to her overflowing inbox. At night, she'd stuff paperwork in her two big, black and worn briefcases and lug them home. It was a wonder Anna's heart could even beat under the weight and pressure of these bags, filled with so much work and responsibility.

On the outside, Anna was powerful, important, and highly competent. She had achieved the success many long for. On the inside, Anna knew she pushed herself too hard. The late night fast food dinners eaten as she continued to work from home, along with too many missed warning signals, and a complete disregard for her body's needs tugged at her soul. Deep inside, she knew she was walking a tightrope, the threads of which were frayed in more than one place. Living on caffeine, fast food, and four hours of sleep each night was taking its toll and she knew, at some point she would have to pay the price. However, she didn't think it would be so soon.

One night at her computer, she started feeling dizzy and light headed. "What's happening to me," she thought as the room spun in circles. She tried to remember when she had last eaten and she felt disoriented. She stood up and her legs buckled, sending her crashing to the floor. For a brief moment, paralyzing fear engulfed her, then she let go and everything went black.

She awoke in the hospital, her eyes landing on her doctor. "What happened to me?" she asked.

"You were in a diabetic coma, and almost died, Anna. You were very, very lucky your colleague found you when she did. You cannot continue to live like this. You have to take care of yourself or next time you won't be so lucky. You're out of the woods for now, but you are going to have to make some serious lifestyle changes. I am referring you to several specialists."

Denial was Anna's first reaction. "There must be some mistake; I couldn't have been in a diabetic coma. I think I just stood up too fast, got dizzy, and bumped my head," she said, trying to convince herself she was in no real danger. When reality set in, Anna was filled with fear and panic. "I almost died! Oh my gosh," she thought, blinking back tears so the doctor wouldn't see.

Later, as she lay in the hospital bed, tears streaming down her face, depressed and defeated, Anna came face to face with her life. "What am I doing to myself?" she wept. "What do I have to show for my life?" she thought, with a deep sense of remorse. "No one at work really cares about me. My life means nothing, no one loves me, and no one would miss me if I died," she thought, with a deep ache in her heart. Sadness overwhelmed her like a heavy blanket engulfing and smothering her, keeping her from rising up and out of her sorrow. "I'm killing myself, and I don't want to die," she moaned. "I want to live, breathe, and feel happiness. I want what other people have," she cried out. She felt so lonely, and her life felt empty and meaningless. "What am I going to do?" she thought, feeling hopeless…

Then, Anna remembered a recent conversation with someone at work. Her colleague, Betty, had shared with Anna how her life and outlook had completely transformed since she started working with a Life Coach. Anna couldn't remember all the details, but Betty had definitely looked happier recently. In fact, she seemed to glow from the inside out and walked with a confidence Anna had never seen in her before.

"When I get out of the hospital, I'm calling Betty to get that coach's name," Anna decided. But the voices of self-doubt in her head were loud. "I'll never be like the Bettys of the world," she thought. "People love Betty, and no one could possibly love me, I don't even love me…" She struggled with the inner conflict between the workaholism she knew well, and what she felt at a deep level might save her life. Then the doctor came back into the room, and Anna knew something had to change.

A few days later, Anna found herself staring at Coach Liz's website. "I'll call her in 10 minutes," she convinced herself. A half hour later, her inner conflict continued. "What if she asks me something I can't answer or I look stupid?" she thought, panicking. She picked up the phone and dialed, then quickly hung up. "Oh, what's the use?" she thought, feeling hopeless. "She's just going to point out the unhealthy things I'm doing, and I don't need to feel bad about myself, or guilty or embarrassed. I don't need that right now! Coaching probably wouldn't work with me anyway."

Then she looked at the website again. This time a phrase caught her eye: "The secret to real and lasting success is in learning to discover and honor who you really are at your core, your Core Heart Essence (CHE™). I will help you gain clarity in all areas of your life. You will learn to make conscious choices that support your CHE™. Let me help you find the real you beneath the stress and pressures of daily living." Intrigued, she picked up the phone again.

"Hello, this is Anna, and I heard about you from a colleague. I'm interested in hearing more about CHE™ and how I can learn to make better choices," she said, weakly.

Coach Liz began with an explanation of Core Heart Essence. "If you were to set aside your roles, responsibilities, "to do" list, the expectations of others, and what you think you "should" be doing, you would uncover who you really are. That essence encompasses your values, gifts, skills, abilities, passions, desires, and the full potential of who you are meant to be. Some people believe God created your CHE™ and that your heart is equipped with a strong inner knowledge about what is right for you at a deep and core heart level. Others believe CHE™ *is* God. It is that knowing voice that whispers in your ear, telling you the right thing to do, if you would only listen. It is that feeling you have, you know, that inner knowing, sometimes hard to explain, that is truth.

"When you live from your CHE™, you set your own course, one that allows you to passionately and completely express who you are. You become *masterfully and brilliantly* in charge of your own destiny, *feeling whole, connected, and inspired.*"

"It sounds interesting," Anna said, feeling excited. "How do I discover my CHE™?"

Coach Liz began her work with Anna by giving her a questionnaire.

"When answering the questions, the first answer that comes to mind is the most important Anna. It usually comes from your heart, before your mind starts telling you your answers are ridiculous, and you become filled with self-doubt. So when responding, try to write down the first thing that comes to mind, and try not to censure your answers."

Anna eagerly awaited the email that contained the 30 questions, but when she read the first few, she felt intimidated. As she started to answer them, she wondered what the coach was trying to uncover.

What do I value, what is important to me?
What are five personal strengths or assets?
What would I do if I knew I could not fail?
What gives me great joy?
To what am I committed?
How would my "heart" describe me?

"I have never thought about these things and I am never going to be able to answer these questions," she thought to herself. Starting to panic, she remembered something Coach Liz had suggested. She closed her eyes and took a few deep breaths and thought about how her heart would describe her. Suddenly, she felt her body tighten, the muscles in her face contract, her breath catch in her throat, and as if a deep floodgate opened, tears spilled out of her eyes and a deep release was set into motion.

Anna knew she had disowned her heart for many years, and the mere act of calling attention to it brought intense feeling. She was depressed and elated at the same time. She felt deeply sorry for herself, for not caring for this vital part of herself, and she knew immediately, intuitively and deeply what she had been doing. She was elated because somewhere inside she felt as if she was seeing a dear and loving friend whom she hadn't seen in years, and the opportunity to visit with that old friend filled Anna with joy.

The rest of the questionnaire seemed to flow easily and Anna found herself finished with the questions with enough time to write in her journal, a treasured new ritual and assignment Coach Liz had given her.

She titled her writing, "What would my core heart essence (CHE™) say to me if she had a microphone and stood on center stage with my full attention? What does my CHE™ want me to know?" She wrote:

"I want you to know how much I love you and miss you. Long ago we were one and now you don't know me at all. I want you to take care of us, loving care of us, eat well, get adequate exercise, sleep, and fresh air, cherish our body, say kind things to us, better yet, say loving things to us, don't work so hard, and find people who love us and who will support us in staying healthy. It's time to let go of the pain and turn the page on a new chapter in our life. Work is important, but not at our expense. We have to make these changes now. Start painting again, find things we love and surround ourselves with them. I don't want you to kill us by neglecting our deep needs. I am here for you and you merely have to remember and think of me. I am your deep wisdom and knowledge and know what is right for us, the keeper of curiosity, innocence, creativity, happiness, passion, and grace. I am where infinite possibility, love, and hope reside, and I store our promising and limitless potential. I will never leave you and I am always here. So connect with me, stay connected, and remember how important this is. When we are connected, everything flows exactly as it should, and you have more to give others and to us. Allow me to speak first, in all things."

Anna put her pen and paper down and closed her eyes. She took it all in, inviting, welcoming, and embracing this newfound connection with herself. She felt softer, vulnerable, and filled with love, yet excited to explore her world with this new inner connection.

This was a revelation and turning point in Anna's life. Now that she could *really* see herself when looking in a mirror, instead of who she thought she should be, she felt more accountable to herself. She felt uneasy when she made decisions that were in conflict with her CHE™, such as saying yes to additional assignments at work, or choosing not to go to the gym. She practiced the new skill of checking in with her CHE™ at specific times during the day. This helped her create conscious inner dialog and make healthy daily choices. Each day she wrote in her journal, "Today I honored my CHE™ by ___" and she filled in the blanks. This helped Anna stay connected and aware of what was important to her.

Anna was elated with her new discoveries, new skills, and life changes as her coaching continued. However, she faced challenges when her life choices did not reflect her CHE™.

Work was overwhelming again. There were pressures from everywhere and Anna found herself back in her old habit of working late hours and bringing work home. Because of her expertise, her boss asked her to complete several additional projects, even though she shared with him that she was making life changes that were important to her.

Anna's boss knew exactly how to manipulate her into doing the extra work, and he had done so for years. After all, he was the highest person in the agency, and it was Anna's job to make him look good. So he worked his angles.

"I'll just do it this weekend," she thought, not wanting to let her boss down and wanting desperately to help others. She heard the voice of her CHE™ but purposely cast it aside. It seemed easy to ignore the commitment she had made to herself and Coach Liz when she felt so needed and important at work.

One week turned into two, and Anna continued to overwork herself. She stopped going to the gym, hurriedly ate unhealthy fast food, and worked late in the evenings. To those on the outside it seemed as if nothing in her life had changed. . .

"I really miss talking with Coach Liz," she thought sadly, as issues came up she wanted to discuss with her. "I'll call Coach Liz later when things calm down, because they really need me at work right now and can not function without me. I'll just do it this one last time... I feel bad about canceling the last two coaching appointments, but this is what I have to do," she thought with resignation.

The longer she put off getting back on track with her program, the easier it became to pretend things were ok...or so she thought.

One night sitting at her desk, Anna was feeling frustrated and stressed. Things weren't coming together and she didn't feel she was doing her best at work. Even though he didn't say it, she could tell her boss was disappointed in her work on the last two projects. Something had changed in Anna. It was as if her heart was no longer in her work. She knew that she was not being effective, and for the first time ever, a growing part of her didn't care.

"What is wrong with me?" she thought with panic and confusion. "I've never done so poorly at work. I feeling like I'm watching myself fail, and I can't stop it. And look at my life," she thought, as she felt a growing depression. "I'm not working out, not coaching, not doing any of the things I said I wanted to do. Worst of all, I'm not honoring my CHE™. I'm such a failure," she thought, as she rested her forehead on her hands and began to cry, pouring out her deep and profound inner struggle in her tears.

The next morning Anna didn't go to work and instead called Coach Liz. "I am feeling so bad Coach Liz. Something has changed in my life. I feel like a failure, like something is very wrong, and I don't know what to do. I don't feel productive anywhere in my life. I am failing at work and I think I'm going to be fired. I can't do my job like I used to. Something has changed. I'm not working out, coaching, or doing any of the things I said I wanted to do for myself. It's weird, but I don't feel like the same person."

After letting Anna pour out her story, Coach Liz provided a possible explanation. "Anna, it sounds like you're not able to resume your old familiar patterns, and the things you did before are not working for you anymore. You are also unable to embrace and follow through on the changes you have made in your life. You seem to be caught between two worlds, one that no longer fits and the other one you are not yet comfortable in."

"That's it exactly! I don't feel like the familiar me anymore. It's like I've changed and nothing works now. It's as if something is stopping me from continuing to over-work like I did before. Even if I want to, I can't do it anymore."

"What do you think is going on with you Anna? What has changed?"

"Something inside me is not allowing me to continue in my unhealthy habits. I wonder if it's my CHE™ trying to stop me from harming myself." Suddenly Anna had a powerful revelation. "It's starting to make sense," Anna said with strength and conviction. "My CHE™ voice is getting stronger, and she is trying to keep me on course and protect me from harming myself!"

"What else is your CHE™ telling you Anna?"

"I'm going to tell my boss that I'm taking better care of myself, and I will not work at the same pace any longer. If that is not ok, I'm going to quit and look for another job. I'm going to stop staying up so late! I'll continue coaching, go back to the gym, see my personal trainer, nutritionist, and massage therapist on a regular basis because those things support me and honor my CHE™. That's what my CHE™ is telling me, and it feels right."

Anna started her commitment by writing on her calendar what her intentions were and when she wanted to accomplish them. She wrote a date to talk with her boss, and marked down days that she would go to the gym.

Coach Liz also gave her homework assignments. "I'd like you to write stream of consciousness with this as the topic: '*What will support me in honoring my CHE?*' Another one I'd like you to write about is, '*What would my life be like if I used the same high standards for excellence in caring for and honoring my CHE™ as I do for work?*'

"And I want you to hold this question in your awareness until we talk again. Just allow the question to enter your mind, and think about it, with no struggle, being open to whatever comes up: **'As I fully honor my CHE™, what am I offering to myself, and to the world?'"**

Anna's connection with her CHE™ continued to deepen and strengthen as she continued her coaching sessions. She attended a workshop to help her gain clarity and create CHE™ action plans in other areas of her life as well. She joined a support group of people also committed to personal growth through honoring their CHE™, and she began speaking in public about the life transforming experiences in her life. She learned how to share herself with others and make true and lasting friendships while supporting and helping others on their journey.

Anna began to look deeply at all areas of her life—relationships, career, spirituality, home life, wealth and prosperity, service to others, family and significant others. In doing so, she learned techniques to help discover her values, visualizing the ideal setting for honoring her CHE™ in each area, writing intentions, goals, sharing with others, and creating collages and paintings depicting her CHE™.

While there continued to be struggles, Anna now had a process through which she filtered and worked through her life challenges. In all things, she worked to honor her CHE™, knowing that in doing so, she was more effective in all areas of her life, had more to offer others, and she was happier and more content than ever before.

***

The woman on the stage looked out at the audience, on the edge of their seats as she told the story of Anna. "If you don't already know my story, Anna is me." A collective gasp issued from the audience. "A year ago, I lay dying on the floor of my study. I remember how frightened and lost I was in my life. What filled my mind then is completely different from the fulfilling internal relationship I have with myself now. I love knowing who I am at my core, and the rich, loving, and vibrant relationship I have with me," she continued with passion. "I am so grateful and fortunate I made this discovery. I hope you, too, will find your CHE™."

As the crowd rose to applaud, she remembered the image she had written of her CHE™ with a microphone on center stage. She smiled as she silently thanked her Core Heart Essence for guiding her to share her story so others could change their lives, too.

Epilogue

This story is based on the life of a real person who, unlike Anna, did not have a second chance to recreate her life. She died that night in her study, and that death ended her ability to live a life that was deeply fulfilling, that honored who she was at her core. The disconnection and lack of positive self-relationship cost her, her life. It was a tragic and unnecessary ending to a life that could have been filled with passion, joy, love, and connection with self and others.

We can learn a lot from Anna's story. How many times during the day, week, month, and year do we sacrifice a deep and meaningful relationship with ourselves for the good of our work? As we get ahead in whatever task we are pursuing, what are we leaving behind? What begins to die within us as we sacrifice our CHE™ more and more? What would it take for you and me to keep this alive for ourselves on a daily basis? How would our lives be different if we stayed connected with ourselves, and in doing so, what would we be offering the world?

Practicing self-care is critical, not only from a physiological standpoint, but also from an emotional, spiritual, and intellectual perspective. Taking exquisite care of yourself acknowledges to you that you are important, that your well-being is a priority, even enough to make sacrifices of time, money, and sometimes, the well-being of other people. Self-care is soul-searching to discover who you are at your core, and then creating a plan to fully support that inner being. It's making choices based on what's good for you, rather than in reaction to what's happening in your world. This is practicing exquisite self care, and it has a far greater, more meaningful, and lasting effect than when you receive kind and caring recognition from others (even though these are wonderful too).

Too often, people seek that care and approval from the outside, adjusting behavior, and a sense of self worth based on the opinions of others. Living like this results in a never-ending quest for approval and acceptance from the outside. We do this with high hopes that somehow this external feedback will transform us on the inside, finally making us good enough. Receiving accolades, and accomplishing tasks we set out to do for external reasons is never enough. Often we are left feeling empty and lost and we quickly begin the search for that illusive sense of "okay-ness" we think we will get if we just try harder or look in different places.

When you create a vibrant and lasting relationship with yourself, you have the opportunity to look deeply at your life, revising decisions made long ago that no longer fit, or that may be preventing you from realizing your unique gifts. You can then truly discover who you are at your core, including what is important to you, and what you value. When this vital connection is made, your life will begin to transform and reflect the real you, rather than squeezing yourself into roles others want you to play.

I invite you to learn from this story and make changes in your life today. Don't allow your life to end without realizing your full potential. What three changes will you begin now?

I encourage you to discover and connect deeply with yourself, as you walk through life. Love, nurture, and more than anything else, develop intense compassion for yourself in all things.

About
Patricia Eslava Vessey

Wellness and Leadership Expert Patricia Eslava Vessey is the President of Integrity Coaching and Training Systems, a professional life coaching, training, and wellness company. With over 30 years experience in leadership and wellness, Patricia provides leadership training, staff development, team building, and wellness & fitness programs to groups and individuals. She helps her clients bring balance to their busy lives, live with passion and purpose—true to themselves while honoring their CHE™, and she supports them in achieving the personal success they desire.

Patricia's career reflects her lifelong passion of helping others realize their full potential through providing social work services to children, families, and others. Much of her career has been in leadership positions, coaching, mentoring, and inspiring others to discover and be their best.

Patricia loves to help others achieve their fitness and wellness goals, while creating meaningful and fun experiences. Her energetic, popular, and creative classes have inspired others for almost 27 years, and they keep coming back for more!

One of Patricia's strongest values is her commitment to lifelong learning, not only academically, but also more richly from life experiences. The cup is always more than half-full for her. She finds and learns from the rich bounty in all situations, especially difficult ones. She believes they are opportunities to learn more about ourselves, grow in understanding and appreciation of our world, and make conscious choices in alignment with what is important to us.

Patricia is passionate about helping others transform limiting beliefs and behaviors into a successful and honoring self-discovery. Doing this fully expresses her CHE™. She believes deeply and passionately in creating a healthy inner life, filled with compassion, love, appreciation, and commitment to self. Creating this strong foundation first, she knows, will help you face any obstacle with confidence, contribute abundantly to the world, and serve as a platform for creating the life experiences you desire. Whether in one of her numerous and varied fitness, wellness, leadership, or other classes, in a coaching relationship, or in a conversation, Patricia's devotion to supporting others is transforming lives.

For more information, visit www.integritylifecoach.com, call 206-459-2898, or email patricia@integritylifeco ach.com.

The Essence of Relationships

By Theresa Swift

I sit here, crying at the news from my beloved friend, Jodi, whose father has cancer and one year to live. I've allowed myself to let the words sink in. Then slowly I start to realize the larger impact on others... How is she doing? What can I do? Will his wife have the support she needs? Even with one year preparation, the finality weighs in the air.

My mind wanders to a conversation I had yesterday. I was invited to author a piece on vibrant and lasting relationships. I am overlapping feelings and new thoughts. "Why am I crying?" I wonder aloud to myself. What makes *my relationship with Jodi* so special—special enough to evoke deep emotion? For the book, I had thought that I might write about the benefits of conflict, the importance of communication, shared values, expression of emotions, or being on the same team. But in the midst of crying and leaning heavily on my sad spirit, something greater poured forth. Much greater. Sharing wisdom on "How to get along together" is good to know, but it is not the *essence* of lasting and vibrant relationships. The immediate possibility of loss brings my values in life to the forefront; the real connections; the real love. I ask myself, "What is the intrinsic glue that bonds relationships?"

As I cry and remain in this dual state of feeling and observing my thoughts, I start to formulate a few things. First, I realize my worries are insignificant. Have you ever noticed that your personal worries disappear when you hear a larger concern? It's the ol' "I thought I was having a bad day, until my neighbor Sally told me about her day. Poor gal!" Bad news, a loss, a significant change, death–all of these threaten safe relationships, the status quo. It brings a jolt of faith, sometimes self-irony and humor about your own worries, but primarily it brings *the present moment* to you.

The new larger importance takes the place of your "now little" worry, and often evokes care, action, and bonding. You move from worry space to care and support. It's an open and compelling invitation to rise above the day-to-day conundrum… a call to value this impermanent thing called life.

Second, what connected me to this beloved friend? Even my terminology "beloved" expresses my affection toward her. There are a zillion people on earth. Yet only a few that you typically connect heart-to-heart, soul-to-soul. I'm sure you have those friends. Someone who knows your words before you say them, or the friend who's been with you through so many experiences, or perhaps someone you haven't seen in years, but when the two of you get together it's like no time has passed. Friendships, relationships that last, not feeling the impact of time. Call it love, spiritual connection, a bond.

What if you had that kind of timeless, priceless relationship bond with your neighborhood, work place, family, community? What if you could somehow stretch that bond you have with a few souls to the breadth of humanity?

Finally, I think about the relationship lifecycle… married for decades, a legacy of children and grandchildren, and various accomplishments in life. What would life be like without a witness to who you are? Vibrant and lasting relationships have people to share ups and downs, join in challenges, point out weaknesses, share in laughter and love, and to be a backbone of support. Lasting relationship members really see *who you are* and are with you as *you are becoming*. Witnessing—your personal presence seeing or knowing—brings both vibrancy and peace into the state of being with another person. A shared experience between people; there won't be another exactly like it.

As I am faced with earthly separation, I'm aware of three essentials for lasting relationships:

1. Embracing the present moment
2. Connecting through heart and soul
3. Revealing self and witnessing others

When integrated, they strengthen your relationships while fortifying your personal essence of life and spirit. Your personal connection with time, with your inner self, and with others are foundational relationship building blocks.

Embracing the Present Moment

What is compelling about the present moment? What comes to mind is true enjoyment, heightened awareness of self and others... that vibrancy of life. The more you live in the present, the higher your "vibrancy of life" meter. You only have a finite time here on earth. Your precious time is better spent on more important things than kicking old past rocks and worrying about future rain drops. Being in the present is a foundation for many life and relationship skills that help you to enjoy your life in a fuller way.

Here's an illustration of the relevance of present moment on self and relationships. One beautiful morning a group of friends met to walk a couple of miles along a nature trail in the mountains to a picnic area for lunch. Once there, they planned to play some badminton, skip a few rocks in the stream, pick berries, laugh together....

As they started out on the trail, Mr. Past stumbled and stubbed his toe on a large rock. He jumped up and down yelling, "Ouch! That stupid rock!" The group halted for a moment and then continued walking, but Mr. Past turned back to kick the rock. "You messed up my shoes! If only you had been on the other side of the path." The group motioned for Mr. Past to rejoin them.

Mr. Past joined the group again, but for the rest of the walk he grumbled about the rock, how his day was now ruined, and that his new shoes were scuffed up. He stayed in that frame of mind most of the day—told others about his mishaps, re-inspected his shoe, wondered if he could have done something to prevent stumbling.

As the group neared the picnic area, Ms. Worree said, "What if we can't find our way back to the car?" She had concerns about going on this trip to begin with, as there could be bears in the area and she didn't want to be "eaten by one." She never saw the beautiful fall foliage because she was pointing to the small cloud in the sky wondering if the group might get struck by lightning or be rained on and catch colds.

For both Mr. Past and Ms. Worree, the beauty of the day was missed. The two were not emotionally in the present and quite unavailable to their friends. The camaraderie and connection was lost. The relationships of the individuals were strained. The present moment was either masked by past "stuckness" or future worries.

Though this is a made-up story, I'm sure you know people in your life who resemble Mr. Past or Ms. Worree. I have seen people turn the past into present agony—reliving day-to-day incidences over and over until it consumed them. Their work suffered, physical health deteriorated, relationships were emotionally empty or tense. What costly "should haves" and "if onlys"! I've also seen people imagine their future way into present burdens. "What ifs" have paralyzed couples from enjoying outings and have broken up "my sunshine" relationships.

A lot of time is wasted fretting about the past or imagining difficult futures. Now don't get me wrong, everyone does this to some extent. However, past or future fretting that starts to become and define you can hinder your present enjoyment, your thoughts, your attitudes, your self and yes, the other people around you.

Truly… what a gift the present holds for you.

MAKE THE PRESENT MOMENT YOUR REALITY

Before moving on from the dimension of time in your life—past, present, future—to engage your heart and soul, and lastly to engage with others, here's the practicality of "the present" dimension applied to daily life.

Think about yourself for a moment. What whisks you away from enjoying the present? With what aren't you comfortable in your own skin? At what times do you not accept circumstances? How do your worries about the future or belabors about the past impact your relationships?

If you have a habit of living in the past or the future, how do you move to living in *the now*? Shifting your mindset, your focus to the present can be done through:

- Awareness
- Choice
- Acceptance

Awareness

Look at your hands. Really notice them—the veins, skin color, nail shape, freckles and so on. Notice your thoughts as you do this. Throw away all judgment. Let thoughts move in and out of your mind freely. Next, notice your body's inner feelings and responses. Is your stomach tight? Wow. Your foot is tapping. How fast is your heart beating? Become aware of how you breathe. Slow down your breathing. Appreciate the fact that you have a body and all its sensory functions. Set aside a few minutes a day to *notice* things, starting with a different area each day–body, emotions, thoughts, breath, senses.

After practicing self-awareness, I invite you to expand your "ad-venture" to awareness with another person: a relationship. The next time you're at lunch with a friend or spouse, notice that person's face, the details, the expression, the smile. Appreciate the hello touch; a handshake, hug, kiss. Enlarge your "circle of attention and listening" and become aware of sounds around you. Listen to the sounds in the room, the air conditioning, the music; see other people near by. Now shrink your "circle of attention and listening" to just the two of you. Pay attention to the person in front of you. Listen with your whole body: ears, eyes, heart, intuition. What's important about the person's conversation *to him or her*? What's important about the conversation *to you*? Let the person know you hear his or her passion, values, importance or feelings. Hear the tone, watch the face expression. Relax. Enjoy. Taste the food flavors. At first it might seem like work, but after awhile the quality of life, enjoyment of intimacy, and being in the present will become second nature.

CHOICE

Let's take Mr. Past as an example for the concept of choice. Rather than rehash the story with his friends time and time again, he could have *chosen* to respond differently. How many hours of enjoyment did he miss by playing his song over and over again? After stumbling over the rock, Mr. Past could have chosen to laugh about it—"Only 10 minutes into our adventure and I already broke in my shoes!" You can consciously choose how to respond to circumstances. In fact, even if you're in the middle of one response, you can change your response midstream.

There's also choice in silence. Silence can imply disinterest, collusion, anger, discomfort, etc. A friend of mine was postponing and ignoring—being silent—about a decision he had to make, so that he wouldn't have to make the decision. Just by my friend's thought and behavior—to do nothing and stall—*he had chosen*. It reminds me of lyrics to a Rush song [Free Will]: "If you choose not to decide, you still have made a choice." Increase your awareness of personal choice in your voice and in your silence.

There's a choice of how and with whom you want to spend your time. At times in my life I've had to cut ties with persons even though I had strong connections and strong feelings. The people that you have in your life, those you have around you, are choices you make. Why live in discord or angst when you can make a choice to change your own behavior, your surroundings, your role models, your peers, your connections? Surround yourself with people you enjoy or those who inspire you to be your best.

ACCEPTANCE

How does acceptance fit in with present moment? Acceptance is like a tree with many sturdy roots. There's acceptance of self, acceptance of others, acceptance of circumstance. As these roots acquire nourishment, the tree continues to grow strong and healthy. So it is with humans too.

SELF

If you don't accept yourself for who you are right now, how does it affect your ability to stay in the present moment? How might it impact your "vibrancy of life" meter? I imagine this self-*un*acceptance could bring various kinds of feelings, such as insecurity, negative outlook, shame, depression, approval-seeking, insufficiency. If you are concerned about self-acceptance, self-image, self-esteem, self-confidence... all that self-stuff, then how easy is it, do you think, to live in the present moment!?

OTHERS

Let's look at another core root. What if you didn't accept others? How might you subsequently react or feel toward them. Perhaps behaviors and attitudes might take the form of criticism, resentment, worry, insult, anger, sadness, disregard, disdain. If a couple is living like this, would you guess that they are enjoying their relationship?

CIRCUMSTANCES

Accepting circumstances—a third core root—enables you to be nimble, make informed decisions, and at times find peace amid chaos. Living in denial, applying selective listening, short-changing the grieving process, blaming, manipulating, and controlling, may be behaviors of people who are having difficulty accepting a specific circumstance. I'm not advocating accepting something that goes against your values, personal rights, safety, etc. Nor does accepting circumstances suggest that you stop dreaming or expressing emotions. However, it is a key factor in being able to live a harmonious life.

I encourage you to become aware of your own roots of acceptance. Every day the tree grows and must deal with its present moment. It may be flexing to windy conditions, stillness, darkness, scorching heat, or heavy rains. When malnourished, insecurity rather than acceptance starts whittling away. Each of us has roots that are strong and some that could use a bit of strengthening.

Make a commitment right now to share your observations about your own roots of acceptance with someone in your life. Discuss what type of nourishment your roots need to build. Prepare by agreeing to create a space between the two of you that is comfortable, non-critical, and safe. This is a time to listen to each other without giving advice. When finished, celebrate your ability to share openly together.

Connecting Through Heart & Soul

Not only is living in the present moment key to a relationship, bringing your authentic core—one's heart and soul—to the day is also essential. I surmise that the quality of connections made when a person is fully whole and authentic are meaningful, do last, and are vibrant.

Engage Your Core

It's sunset. The sky is a grey-blue sheet of marble, each cloud etched with red-gold light. Glimmering orange light magnificently reflects upon the lake ahead. The dark, still water has reeds as tall as me forming the banks. A goose slaps the water with its wingtips as it flies just above the glassy surface, heading to join the others gathered as nightfall approaches.

Here's where I gather my inner strength. Here's where I engage my core. My gratitude, happiness, and wholeness awaken again in me as I see the beauty around me. The more I surround myself with the world's beauty shown in nature, movement, stillness, contrast … the closer to my true self I become. As I take time for myself, do the things that make me happy, the more I also become receptive to what the world and other people have to offer. I feel connected to the earth and creation. When I'm in this state, I am more able to reach out with love in my relationships. I can appreciate those special connections with people throughout each day more freely. I'm able to better reflect on the day, gain insights, and have a sense of ease and well-being in my core. I'm in a state of gratitude.

When you feel grateful, your life becomes easier. Imagine living in a state of gratitude and love during the majority of your life… at work, at the grocery store, with your spouse, your children, on the phone. Do you ever notice when you appreciate the world around you, your family, your job, and so on, how much more *giving* people are in return? It's an upward spiral that touches everyone around you.

When you're in a relaxed, easy state of mind, it's as if life just keeps going your way. Perhaps running brings that ease to your soul; maybe it's immersing yourself into the depths of your painting; possibly music takes you there; perhaps prayer rejuvenates your spirit. The manner of bringing you in touch with your own heart and soul is unique to you. Even this uniqueness adds to your personal, delightful, strong authentic core. It is from this place that connections to others have more meaning.

Make Connections

What is it about that special connection between two people? Upon first meeting someone, do you hear a little voice, or intuition, that connects you?

There's a bond between people. Sometimes you "hit it off" with someone new because of the various things in common. Other times, it's that sense or energy about a person that brings closeness, comfort, affinity, attraction. At times the bond can be felt strongly, other times it's weaker. Some people have a physical feeling, like an invisible cord is tied from their center to another person's center. Sometimes you are so into your own self, life, fears, biases, that you miss the connection altogether.

Attend to Life Enhancers and Life Exhausters

There are people who are life enhancers, those whom you feel good to be around, those who bring out the best in you. Natural life enhancers are the friendships that develop into "lasting relationships." By "lasting" I don't mean staying together based on fear: "because I won't find anyone else"; "I don't have money to be independent"; or "I signed a document." Yes, relationships of these sorts last, but with those thoughts I doubt the "vibrancy of life" meter is pegged! By "lasting relationships" I mean staying together out of free will, that you *want* to be together and enjoy each other's company. Sure there are ups and downs, but there's a naturalness to this kind of "lasting." Special friendships or happenstances are not taken for granted. When you meet or have those life enhancers in your life, take the care to nurture those relationships.

On the other hand, there are people who are life exhausters. The person may be a great guy or gal, but the interactions between you may not be positive or happy; instead the connection is marred with tension or anger. Put your awareness hat on and notice your own signals and the relationship signals. For instance, are you feeling aggravated after each encounter, obligated to spend time with someone, or increasingly upset? Be aware of the affect a new person has on you, your positive or negative thoughts, the ease and naturalness of the relationship space, the joy in your voice, smile on your face, or tightness in your stomach. The initial connection may be strong and intense, or barely a murmur of vibration. Listen to what your senses, intellect, and spirit have to tell you.

When you're in a state of grace or awareness, I believe you're more able to connect and relate better with other people. The reflection and time you take to connect to your personal happiness and re-vivify your heart and soul, supplies peace, joy, and wholeness. That in turn naturally gets showered on everyone with whom you come into contact. It's like a 4th of July sparkler. Your genuineness and gratitude create sparks and sets off other sparklers around you. In turn, each sparkler lights more sparklers. Imagine the field of light that you can create from your own sparkler—a sight to behold! It starts from your core, your heart and soul, and then expands to other people, your relationships. Ignite your relationships and connect with others on that level of heart-to-heart, spirit-to-spirit.

Revealing Self and Witnessing Others

You've taken steps to live more fully in the present moment and have now ignited your personal sparkler, from which other sparklers have been lit through relationship. A lasting spark can then be formed through rekindling…

To maintain an intimate and lasting relationship with someone else, you have to reveal who you are—allow yourself to be seen and known by others. AND you have to acknowledge the person you see in front of you. This process of revealing and witnessing kindles a deeper relationship.

When you allow your layers of self to be seen, the more you can connect with another human being on a deeper level. This way of being with one another—this intimacy—starts to encourage more and more of your natural beauty, heart, and purpose. Relating to each other at this depth of knowing may be joyous, awe-inspiring, warm, intense, soft, or powerful. Revealing of oneself can also carry with it risk, vulnerability, and fear.

Reveal

A close friend of mine, Jay, had always dreamed of this kind of closeness and intimacy in his life. A few years ago, Jay fell deeply in love with a woman named Niejé. He would draw her near and reveal a bit about himself, and a bit more, and his relationship began to soar. He was on a cloud! Life couldn't be better. He told me the happiest days of his life were when he was with Niejé. Jay said he never told anyone many of the things he shared with Niejé. He allowed her to see, to know, and to love him. Who he was, who he is, and who he was becoming. In my life, I've hardly seen a happier, beaming man.

There came a point when Jay got scared. As he revealed more of who he was to Niejé, he started to let his inner voice get out of hand. The more he cared for her, the more he heard his "what ifs". "What if she learns about the 'real me' and doesn't like me? What if she leaves me?" His negative, self-critical, inner voice played havoc with his mind and confidence. Rather than receive the closeness, safety, and love within the relationship, he started to push it away. This behavior confused and devastated Nieje. She too had been revealing more of her "self," her heart. But Jay found ways to tear the relationship down and retreat. When I last spoke to him, Jay decided that he'd rather live a life of small talk and acquaintances. He chose this eventual destiny.

My heart wrenches when I think of the story of their love. For years Jay wanted and yearned for a truly intimate relationship, but when the opportunity came, he let his fears overshadow love and connection.

You each have areas of yourselves that are endearing to your loved ones, and other areas that may not be the most stellar. Both your "good and bad" are what make you who you are today. You are *living* life, after all! When you become closer and more intimate with another person, various areas get revealed, shared, and exposed. That's natural. When two people care for each other and are able to share deep experiences with one another, a tighter mutual understanding emerges.

What does it take for a deeper, vibrant connection? Revealing of self and witnessing of others. As seen with my friend Jay, before he can be ready for an intimate and lasting relationship, he'll need to love himself and grow in his personal acceptance.

WITNESS

A desire to be seen and known starts at a young age. Think about the last time you watched children at play. One sister is swinging on the swing set. You hear, "Look Daddy. Watch me!", as the child jumps off the swing into the sand. Her sister races to get the empty and slowing swing. "My turn. Push me. Watch what I can do!" Witnessing can be either active or passive—doing or being. It involves hearing about or seeing something happen, or experiencing it first hand within yourself or with another person. Seeing—involvement—acknowledgement… three key parts of witnessing and building lasting relationships.

SEEING

What do you want someone to see and know about *you*? See my life, achievements. See my greatness. See my strengths, my attempts, my creations. Know my uniqueness, my special traits. Know my heart and the things I did, the person I am, on this earth. You want to feel like someone really knows you and sees you for who you are. Or as The Goo Goo Dolls sing [Iris], "I just want you to know who I am."

INVOLVEMENT

A friend of mine told me today that he misses his girlfriend. They used to live together and she's now living in another city for work. He misses sitting together, talking together, her support, eating dinner together, helping her, touching… being involved in her life and she in his life in a variety of ways.

Often times, involvement is simply *being there*; being in the same physical location together. A sharing of common experience or understanding without words. Perhaps a non-verbal involvement—a smile, a wink from across the room—that says I understand or we're in this together or both share in the joke. Sometimes a word of validation or understanding lets the other person know that you're involved.

Acknowledgment

Here's an example of acknowledgment through the revealing and witnessing process. Kate finished speaking to an audience of 500 about courage and love within communities. Her brother, Tom, blurted his feelings, "Wow! That was an awesome speech you just gave." Kate responded, "It wasn't a speech, it was a poetry reading." Her brother then said, "I really heard the passion in your voice and saw how much 'teams built on integrity and care' mean to you. It moved me."

Kate revealed part of her inner self through her poetry. Tom first witnessed Kate by attending the event and by being present. He then praised her with "awesome". By not being attached to the outcome (not defensive about her response), he avoided a possible argument with Kate (poetry reading vs. speech correction). He then turned inward to listen to his heart, saw who his sister was being, what she was doing, and then acknowledged her on a more specific and intimate level. Genuinely connecting to someone's feelings, purpose, risk, or character really gives meaning to an acknowledgment.

Relationship Essence

The thought of losing Jodi's father was a strong reminder to me to value my relationships on this earth. Treasuring and strengthening my personal connection with time, my self, and with others, is the essence of lasting and vibrant relationships. Each of you can proactively do this by:

- Spending more time living in the present moment through awareness, choice, and acceptance
- Connecting to your inner self—heart and soul—by finding and spending time doing what makes you happy and at peace
- Revealing your heart to others and witnessing others' lives

Alignment to the present moment brings serenity to individuals, and harmony and vibrancy to relationships. Connection with one's heart and soul leads to deeper gratitude and authenticity. Revealing and witnessing encourages a fuller relationship.

My belief, and one that is continually reinforced just by the nature of life, is to nurture relationships. *Do not take relationships and love for granted.* Your heart and soul is an ever-flowing well of inner peace and outward warmth, radiating like the early rays of sunlight caressing the earth as it moves across the land. Connect with others from this place of love as you go forward each day, and cherish each moment.

About
Theresa Swift

Theresa Swift is a personal coach who specializes in relationships, lifestyle changes, and business success. In all of these areas, she is passionate about her business motto of "staying true to oneself." This means different things to different people—perhaps reaching specific goals, getting energized through life's passions, or finding more balance in life.

You can hear Theresa say relationships need all the support they can get in this day and age. Hence, she believes in being an active part of the solution. Good relationships are important through all walks of life—family, business, community. Theresa has had her share of relationship "ups and downs"—beautiful experiences and painful disappointments. Outside of formal education, her primary lessons on relationships were learned through family, work, love, and ballroom dance partnerships. Whether laughing, crying, smiling, angry, or sad in relationships, she lives life fully!

With an extensive background in organizational dynamics, change management, and project management, Theresa formed a consulting and coaching company, Swift Resolve Coaching. Theresa is a graduate of the Core Coaching Program (Coaches Training Institute) and a certified recovery coach (Crossroads Coaching). She holds an M.S. in Organizational Dynamics (University of Pennsylvania) and an M.S. in Mechanical Engineering (University of CA-Berkeley). She is a certified six-sigma black belt (Intuit) and a graduate of GE's Technical Engineering Leadership program. Theresa also worked throughout Europe and the US with top business leaders while on GE's Corporate Audit Staff.

Theresa is a natural teacher, easily sharing what she has learned in life and business. She also enjoys competitive ballroom dancing, as well as music, travel, and the outdoors.

A Thousand Fibers, A Sympathetic Thread: Caring About the Happiness of Others

By Kenneth Piazza Malchiodi

"A LEGACY TO OTHERS YOU HOLD DEAR IS THAT YOU CARED."
~ KENNETH PIAZZA MALCHIODI

Six years ago our son Bobby's first child, Mason, was born. From all indications, Mason was a normal little boy with a cheerful smile. However, shortly after his first birthday, feeling that he wasn't developing at what was expected and normal for his age, his parents took him to the doctor to see what was causing his slow progress.

After numerous physical examinations and DNA testing, it was revealed that Mason has a rare genetic disorder called Angelman Syndrome (AS). "Angels" are cognitively disabled and the development of speech is not likely. Typically, language consists of 4-5 indiscriminate words. "Angels" have a happy demeanor, although according to the "experts" they don't or can't show emotions. They have a short attention span, and require 24-hour lifelong care. Although there are estimated to be between 1,000 and 5,000 cases of AS in North America, experts now believe that thousands of Angelman Syndrome cases have gone undiagnosed or misdiagnosed as Cerebral Palsy, Autism, or other childhood disorders. At present, there is no cure for AS.

Five years ago, our family spent a week at the beach in South Carolina. Despite the heat, the days were filled with all the joy you could have spending time with your grown children and their families.

During the week, Mason had his grandpa's full attention in the beach house. I would lie on the floor next to his pad and blanket and hold him, trying to assist him in holding different toys. Mason has ataxia of gait and tremulous movement of limbs, which make it difficult for any concentration of activity when playing with him. At times he will hold onto me and not want to let go. His behavior uniqueness includes frequent laughter and smiling and an easily excitable personality, often with hand flapping movements.

I enjoyed the opportunity of establishing some type of a meaningful relationship, even though the chances were slim because of the disorder.

When I was with him on the floor and we were touching, I felt a tremendous amount of love. He spoke to me with his eyes and was able to convey to me what he needed many times that week. When I entered the room Mason was in, he would become excited and try to reach me, mostly by crawling to me.

At the end of the vacation, his dad placed Mason in his carrier seat. I followed with some luggage and stood smiling at Mason. As I had numerous times during the week, I told him, "Grandpa and Grandma love you." He smiled and as tears rolled down my face, I noticed Mason starting to weep. Oh, what emotions I had as I walked away, slowly waving and throwing kisses to him. So much for the "experts."

Mason is now six years old and took eleven steps on his own as his special needs teacher and his parents watched. This is an accomplishment and hopefully will lead to him being more on his own.

Showing compassion and empathy to Mason and other special needs youngsters and adults is easy in the sense that I want to help them by being with them. Mason senses his grandpa being with him, talking to him, and caring for him. What, if anything, he understands, I don't know. Having him smile and hold onto me is a sense of fulfillment. It appears that it satisfies his needs considering his capacity, and in his way, he feels content and secure.

Isn't this what life is about? To show compassion, empathy, and most of all, love for mankind in our relationships—all of our relationships? To give of one's self is vital to each of us in existence. If I can give a kind word or action to someone, that not only makes me feel that I have helped, but makes the recipient feel they are not forgotten and are appreciated.

Why have an empty heart, when your heart can be full of love and kindness for someone else? Real love is caring about the happiness of another person, giving of your self to help the other person, regardless of who, what, or where they are in their lives. Receiving is part of the equation, but not giving causes relationships to crumble.

Gain Respect, Build Trust, Show You Care

The first gift you can give others who you want to establish a relationship with is respect. This is first because respect establishes trust, an essential requirement to a vibrant and lasting relationship. We must learn to cooperate with one another to gain respect and better understanding, share information, and exchange ideas.

Opportunities to give of yourself happen when you least expect them. My wife, Pat, and I were on a tour with forty other tourists. Most people don't get to really know you for several days, and the contact is mainly very casual with a possible hello, where are you from, etc. We toured on a regular tour bus, which has comfortable seats for two.

Getting on the bus the first day, I noticed a tall, lanky man stretched out in a seat with his legs extended to the window as he was looking at several maps across his body. He was very quiet and didn't speak to anyone boarding. At our first pit stop at a travel center, he spoke briefly to a woman who had been sitting in front of him, but it was a quick conversation and then they appeared to go their separate ways. Again, while re-boarding, he proceeded to stretch out, taking up both sides of the seat and looking at his maps. It was very obvious he wasn't concerned with anyone on the bus.

The first four days the man would walk with the lady on stops. But they rarely exchanged words, nor did they really speak to anyone in the group. They both appeared to be very depressed, especially the man, who was approximately sixty-five years of age, neatly and casually dressed in blue jeans. He always appeared to be enthralled with the maps, again not speaking to anyone. While eating evening meals with the group, he and the lady hardly spoke to one another or anyone else in the group, although most of the other tourists, including my wife and I, tried to sit with different people each evening.

Early on the fifth day, with a light drizzle and 50-degree temperature, we had stopped in a village surrounded with water. Everyone walked around for an hour and met back at the bus as scheduled. After the head count by the tour director, he reported we were missing one person.

Since my wife and I had been sitting across the aisle, one row back, I noticed the empty seat that belonged to our quiet man. The lady was sitting in her seat and she ended up talking to the tour director. She identified herself as the man's wife.

I volunteered with two other men to search for him. I remembered seeing him headed toward an area surrounded by warehouses and commercial fishing boats moored along several docks when I had gotten off the bus earlier. The tour director identified the man as Paul, husband of the lady he had been seen with during the trip.

After twenty minutes of searching in the rain and wind, with no umbrella, I located Paul. I found him staring into the river water at the edge of the pier. I felt, based on what I had observed for several days, that he was possibly depressed, so I didn't want to startle him. At that moment he appeared to be in a trance.

When approaching him, slowly, I spoke softly to him by saying, "P-a-u-l," very slowly. He didn't answer at first.

On the third attempt, and within reach of his left side, he turned to me and said, "Hi."

I said, "My name is Ken, one of your touring buddies."

He replied, "Yea, I know."

I explained that the bus was leaving and we were looking for him to rejoin us. He turned to me and we slowly walked back to the bus, never exchanging any communication.

When arriving back, I noticed the other men had already returned. I proceeded to sit at my seat and Paul returned to his. After sitting down he told his wife he was all right and took a nap.

At the first stop after this occurrence, he and his wife walked off away from the group and returned several hours later, holding hands and smiling. It was very obvious they were happier than they had been since the trip started.

Later that evening, our group gathered for dinner. As Pat and I entered the ballroom area, Paul and his wife, Jane, approached us and introduced themselves to us, asking if we would join them at their table. Paul said, "Thanks for finding me this morning. I really appreciate it."

"So do I," said Jane. "Things will work out."

Paul proceeded to discuss the trip in detail and that they were looking forward to the remainder of the trip. It was rather interesting to find out that they were highly educated people and were actively involved in their church. We had a very enjoyable evening, as we seemed to have similar interests.

Paul couldn't do enough for us from the time we were greeted to four hours later when we returned to our room. Had we been heavy drinkers we would have needed help getting back to our room. He would try to get us more food during the meal, as well as wine.

Nothing was mentioned about that morning's situation.

The following morning Paul and Jane again greeted us at breakfast, which was a breakfast eater's delight. Had we allowed it, they would have served us all morning.

After breakfast we headed onto the bus and continued the tour. For the next several days, I was always welcomed with a hug and a "thanks" from Paul and Jane.

Our last day on the tour, we said our goodbyes to everyone. Paul and Jane hugged us both and thanked us for being "nice people."

Early the next day our group was taken to the airport. We all went our separate ways. Two hours later I noticed a man running through the crowded airport and as he got closer, I recognized Paul. He approached and gave me a big smile and hug and began to cry, again saying, "Thanks for everything. You will never know." Running through the crowd was difficult, especially with the balcony filled with armed military and police covering the perimeter of the terminal, as this had occurred three weeks after the war started in Iraq and we were in a European country. Yes, all eyes were on Paul. He was so happy I don't believe anything fazed him.

He said, "Keep me in your prayers as I know you will."

I said, "Bless you both. Keep in touch."

Paul's appreciation toward me for showing compassionate comfort to him at a time when he needed it from a concerned person made him realize that another human being was concerned for his well-being and reawakened his relationship with Jane and his family.

Giving the gifts of sensitivity, honesty, and gentleness to Paul at a pivotal time in his life, gave him additional time to appreciate what life still has to offer him at his age. Feelings are unique in each relationship. Empathy shown at his time of need, offered by another human—me—gave me the fortunate opportunity to connect and try to understand the feelings involved.

Showing empathy toward Paul in this situation didn't mean I approved of his behavior, but that I was trying to understand it and help him reconnect. I believe Paul was at a period in his life, recently retired, being lonely, puzzled on his future, and disconnected from communication with Jane and his family, therefore leading to his depression.

Listening intently to conversations at the dinner table gave me the feeling he was not able to communicate with others as in the past, and became withdrawn and insecure.

Paul said to me that, "Being genuine cannot be faked." He sensed that I was a genuine person from the time I spotted him at the water's edge. I had gained his respect and trust by my showing him that I cared.

To observe someone after you have assisted them in their dilemma or provided just a moment of kindness when they feel their lives are topsy turvy is satisfying. It's also an opportunity to stop and reflect on the happiness you have provided and what could be done in future experiences.

Caring with Sensitivity and Unconditional Love

Another gift you can give to establish trust in a relationship is to be sensitive to what another person might be feeling. Many people who are in need are fearful of the consequences of revealing themselves, even when it is family or a friend. But those same people will often open up to someone who is perceptive of their needs, even when they are strangers. Offering a sense of warmth, being careful with facial expressions and gestures, listening to voice tone, and making eye contact opens up lines of communication. This builds rapport. In the case of Mason, as many limitations as he has, he knows when he is with someone who cares.

Unconditional love is showing sensitivity toward others without any concern with how that looks or what is returned from the other being in the relationship. Many relationships are avoided or fail because people do not love unconditionally; they do not accept others for who and what they are. Placing restrictions or conditions on the other person in a relationship impedes the growth of the relationship, if not destroying it altogether.

Offering unconditional love relieves the recipient of fear of rejection or criticism from others and allows them the opportunity to feel wanted, feel warmth, caring, and an increase in self-esteem, self worth, and love.

On the other side, so many people live their lives to please others rather than living their own lives honestly. By doing so, they have difficulty having lasting relationships or continue to nurture mediocre connections.

Caring Through Service to Others

"HOW RARE AND WONDERFUL IT IS THAT IN A FLASH OF A MOMENT WE REALIZE THAT WE HAVE MADE A DIFFERENCE IN THE LIFE OF ANOTHER."
~ ANTHONY P. WITHAM

Seeing people for what they are and where they came from is not an issue for those who want to serve others.

Growing up in New Jersey, I was fortunate as I had many opportunities over the years to observe and be mentored by people who served our community with unselfishness and were involved in order to help mankind. From little league coaches to volunteer firemen and rescue squad members risking their lives for a safer community, the people I looked up to gave me the desire to share my self by involvement. They set the example to care. In the end their desires to help others made the world a better place for many.

Bob, the secretary of my board of trustees at the hospital I worked at as President/CEO had battled cancer for over ten years. During that period he had many surgeries and special treatments at another hospital 90 miles away. He never complained during that period. Although he was financially well off, he was a humble man of integrity, and a good friend. After a long and brave battle, he had weakened and lost his appetite, and was admitted in early summer to our hospital. During his stay, he would joke with staff and watch cartoons, despite his chronic pain.

One afternoon, we discussed life in general, nothing serious, but light and memorable. He emphasized the importance of spending time with family more than business, which was something he felt he had failed to do earlier in his career.

He said to me, "All the many years of travel, including a trip around the world, I have always paid my way and always had someone expect something in return in terms of monetary worth. Yet all the time we have been friends, and you a confidante, you have treated me with the greatest respect, and never asked for anything in return. You are a true friend, and I wish you well."

Bob passed away two days later, leaving behind many memories.

Because of occupational involvement as a police officer and working in the health care industry, plus my own life experiences, I realize how precious life is. Life is too short to neglect the opportunity to give aide when needed.

We have many opportunities to be involved with helping other people in our lifetime. Our desire to assist others must be void of selfishness or glory if we are to get true satisfaction out of helping someone in need.

If someone feels better than when I found them, I get enormous satisfaction and a sense of accomplishment. We make many choices each and every day. My choice is to help someone in a time of need. The result is everlasting, both for the recipient and for myself.

In Caring, Expect Nothing

"CARING DEEDS,
A HELPING HAND,
THOUGHTS THAT SHOW
ONE UNDERSTANDS...
THE WORLD IS A BETTER PLACE TO LIVE
BECAUSE OF KINDNESS OTHERS GIVE."
~ CONSTANCE PARKER GRAHAM

While on a trip to Washington, D.C. in the early spring of 1983, I took an afternoon to see the Vietnam Veterans Memorial. It had been dedicated the previous year. The wall was not in sight as I walked quite a distance from across Constitution Avenue. Suddenly, I was looking down about ten feet, not realizing I was actually walking on the top of the supporting wall of the Memorial. As I came to the end and turned to look at the front, I was overwhelmed by its size: 246 feet and over ten feet high.

The day was hot, humid, and beautiful. Looking at the black marble wall and the glare from the sun was memorable, especially seeing hundreds of people along the face of it, taking pictures, doing rubbings (etching the marble with pencils) of combatants who perished during the war, placing memorabilia and flowers at the base of the wall. Each of these cherished artifacts are catalogued and preserved.

Names of combatants are listed chronologically. While doing several rubbings of men I knew from the past and basic training, I was approached by two men who had lost multiple limbs and had been having difficulty doing their respective rubbings. Between the two men, I did fifteen names of men who were part of their outfits in Vietnam. They placed a rose and flag below each row.

By the time I finished, I had taken my jacket and tie off, and had rolled up my sleeves. At least I had two arms and two hands, as well as two legs and feet on which to stand. The men I helped weren't as fortunate. They were sitting on planks attached to rollers, using sticks and the stumps of legs to move around.

Three other men in wheel chairs soon joined us. I helped with over three dozen rubbings for them. While I was doing the rubbings, they talked among themselves. We exchanged names and hometowns, which led to small talk, then to long, drawn out discussions about the war. They were all depressed men in their late thirties and had no outlook of success in the future. They all had major health problems on top of the loss of limbs. We exchanged views on God, which was very interesting, considering the bitterness they had toward life, authority, and mainly, politicians.

After nearly four hours, I told them to wait by the wall and I would get some food for us. I found a deli and bought each of the men a foot long Italian sub sandwich, with sodas. When I returned, they seemed to cheer up. They thought I wouldn't return. They were happy and telling jokes. I had the subs cut in small pieces for them to handle. They were amazed that someone was considerate to them because of their disabilities.

They couldn't remember my name so they called me "Talon," for claw of an animal. After eating we read from Psalms in the Bible and one of the guys read from his Torah. I spent another hour with them, listening and trying to make sense of their losses. All of them, Stephen, Peter, Andrew, Mike, and Terry appreciated the time I spent with them. They all had something major in common besides grief, and that was the forming of new friendships, and some "Jersey Boy named Talon" reaching out to them.

They came from different states, but promised to come each Fourth of July and meet at "The Wall."

I communicated with Peter, as he was able to write. But after three years I never heard from him again. In those years the group had met every year as promised. Although I haven't heard from Peter in years, I will always remember that afternoon of relationship with my new friends.

Service unto others provides an opportunity to realize we may have more in common with those around us than we imagined. We can do it in our every day lives by putting our best foot forward and being sensitive and respectful of others in need regardless of race, color, or creed.

The number one need I find with people is not to understand, but to be understood. Empathy can be painful when we see suffering in others, whether physical or emotional. But empathizing allows each of the people in a relationship to exchange ideas, solve problems, and in many cases, provides the opportunity to help someone in need. Having the willingness to be sensitive to the pain and needs of others and making an attempt to see and experience their world from another perspective is very fulfilling.

Being an effective listener is imperative when communicating with empathy. As the Greek philosopher Epicteus said, "God gave man two ears, but only one mouth, that he might hear twice as much as he speaks." Showing you care by hearing and being sensitive is rewarding to your self as well as those to whom you are directing that care.

Looking back to that day at The Wall, I realized that I had completely lost myself in the moment. I did not have an expectation that I could change the reality of their lives. But I cared deeply for each of them, and for all those affected by their story. And for at least an afternoon, those soldiers *knew* that someone cared. Whether or not we connected for a lifetime, our relationship was vibrant in its simplicity. They are gone, but not forgotten.

A Thousand Fibers, A Sympathetic Thread

"WE CANNOT ONLY LIVE FOR OURSELVES. A THOUSAND FIBERS CONNECT US WITH OUR FELLOW MEN; AND AMONG THOSE FIBERS, A SYMPATHETIC THREAD, OUR ACTIONS RUN AS CAUSES, AND THEY COME BACK TO US AS EFFORTS." ~ HERMAN MELVILLE

In my experience, respect, trust, sensitivity, and service to others are the four pillars of vibrant and lasting relationships. These are the fibers that show that we care. These are the threads that connect us, no matter who we are or how we meet.

There are additional things you can do to build relationships—be sincere, be genuine, be consistent, have an open attitude, be honest… the list goes on. However, if you look at each of these, they all lead back to one of those four pillars.

If someone feels better than when I found them, I get satisfaction and a sense of accomplishment. I make many choices each and every day of my life. My choice to help someone at a time of need, I believe is everlasting, for both of us.

> Do all the good you can,
> By all the means you can,
> In all the ways you can,
> In all the places you can,
> At all the times you can,
> To all the people you can,
> As long as you can.
> ~John Wesley

About
Kenneth Piazza Malchiodi

As an author, life and spiritual coach, public speaker, and entrepreneur, Kenneth Piazza Malchiodi integrates his extensive management, leadership, and entrepreneurial experience over the past forty years into his coaching business.

In addition to a background in law enforcement, a CEO in Hospital Administration, and his work in Human Resources, Ken has owned several businesses. His experience has also included working with young adults, management and business professionals in substance/drug abuse, and as a speaker presenting self improvement and personal growth topics. The latter two are also primary goals in his coaching sessions.

A self-professed, self-improvement junkie, who has sold self-improvement books through mail order for years, Ken's motive is to improve the lives of others, believing that we should love what we do, and do what we dream in our short journey in life.

The way you look at yourself and how you live your life through spiritual insights are significant aspects of his coaching. In regards to relationships, Ken believes putting love and respect first is imperative.

A long time Ohio Buckeye resident, Ken has found a place in warmer climes, close to the ocean in North Charleston, South Carolina, where he and his wife, Pat, reside and he continues coaching and writing.

Ken is also working on a book, "Relationships, Et cetera" and a historical novel, "Westward Migration." He continues his studies in coaching with Comprehensive Coaching University, and is a member of the American Association of Christian Counselors.

To contact Ken, send an e-mail to malchiodiken@yahoo.com

Stormy Relationships:
The Lessons of Hurricane Katrina

I am proud to say that I was born and raised in New Orleans, Louisiana. My life has been filled with Mardi Gras fun (it's not just what you see on MTV), seafood, jazz music, and a deep sense of the joy of life. My parents are both from the Mississippi Gulf Coast, about 45 minutes from the French Quarter, where the beach, the sun, and the laid back life provide the best that life has to offer.

As a child, I survived Hurricanes Betsy and Camille and learned by experience to get out of the way of a Category 5 storm. So, on Saturday, August 27th, 2005, my husband Rudy and I packed up our two children, Ethan who was 12 and Jolie who was 8, and our cat Mrs. Sippy, and started our evacuation adventure.

We knew the drill, as we had evacuated from our Coastal Mississippi town of Bay St. Louis twice before. We took a small suitcase each, our laptop computers, and client files, and packed my Jeep Cherokee as if we were going on a weekend trip. In my husband's VW Passat we loaded the more important stuff: the binder that we keep all of the papers like immunization records, social security cards, and school records in; the plastic bin full of pictures; and all of my photo albums. I remember wishing that my husband liked big trucks instead of small cars so that we could have taken more with us.

Each of the children was allowed one small box to take their very special treasures with them. Jolie took a dance trophy, her build-a-bear, her CDs, and her rosaries. Ethan took his Karate Medals, his CDs, his rosaries, and his ample collection of Pokemon cards. We all had a good laugh at how similar their boxes were. We also allowed them to bring all of their dance gear and Karate gear. Needless to say, Rudy's car was packed.

We didn't really do much to our home to prepare it for the storm. The house we left was an old family home where some of my most cherished childhood memories were born. Over 100 years old, the craftsman style shotgun cottage sat on the highest point on the Gulf of Mexico, at least five blocks from a beach front cliff. It had never been flooded in its history. Most importantly, it survived the infamous Hurricane Camille in 1969 without a scratch.

As our small caravan drove away from our home of the past five years, a house that had been in my family for 70 years, the place where I spent summers and holidays with my loving family throughout my childhood, I was overcome with sadness. I felt as if I was forgetting something and could not figure out what it was. Somehow, I just knew things would never be the same. In retrospect, I now know exactly what I was missing. I was missing saying goodbye to the people in my life. People like the teachers who taught my children, the clerks at the Winn Dixie, my hairdresser, and my Palates instructor. People like my neighbors, my friends, and my family. I took for granted that I would see them all again once we returned home, that they would all still be there and life would go on in the same wonderful way. I took it for granted, and I took them for granted.

We left Rudy's car at the house of my friend and client, Nancy Johnson, in Hattiesburg, Mississippi, thinking that an hour and a half north of the coast was a safe distance for our precious cargo. We continued on to Gatlinburg, Tennessee. For us, evacuations are like mini-vacations and my kids had never been to the Great Smoky Mountains before. We had a great time hiking in the mountains and being together as a family away from home that weekend.

On Monday, when Katrina's eye passed directly over Bay Saint Louis, I knew we would not be able to return home, at least not for a while. As we watched the horror of the storm from our hotel room, the pictures of the chaos in New Orleans started to dominate the TV. We felt an intense desire to be in touch with the important people in our lives, our family and friends.

We tried my mother who refused to evacuate and had told me she was staying at a friend's house that she thought was safe.

We tried my Dad, who called me early Sunday morning and left a message that he and his wife were trying to get out, but that the traffic was terrible and he wasn't sure how far they would get. We started trying to call our best friends, Megan, Owen, and their three boys Bo, Hunter, and Myles, who we knew were safe and had gone to Florida for their evacuation adventure. We tried my sister-in-law, who had her three kids on I-10 in her Suburban stuck in traffic the last time we spoke to her late Sunday night. She could not reach my brother, who is a Ship's Captain and was en route to Africa in the middle of the Atlantic. We desperately tried every number in both our cell phones, which had become useless as the phone switches were down in our home area. We tried, and tried, and tried. We could not reach anyone and they could not reach us. We were isolated from the important people in our lives when we needed each other the most.

As the death and destruction unfolded on national TV, we honestly didn't know if any of our loved ones were still alive. The fear, the enormity of the situation, and the isolation consumed us. We said many prayers that day and asked that God grant us the wisdom and strength that we were surely going to need. Rudy and I knew that we would need to be strong. We both knew that we would need to approach this in a manner that would not escalate the situation into an even bigger drama. It was already huge.

I asked myself what I might do to guide one of my clients who might be in this situation. It came to me in a flash of intuition. We would use the coach approach to guide us through this dark time. So, while our kids were swimming in the motel pool, Rudy and I sat down together and made a list of our values and what was really important to us. We worked on our individual lists and our list as a couple. We decided that we would filter every decision we made from that moment on through our values list so as to not get confused about what to do.

On Wednesday, we went to a coffee shop to check e-mail. We found an e-mail from my mom, who was in a motel in Greenville, Alabama with her best friend Deb and Deb's mother, Miss Evelyn, who was 84. We drove the nine hours to meet them that day. What a relief it was to know that my mother was alive. But to actually put my arms around her was a moment of joy that I will never forget. The joy soon turned to worry as my 67-year old mother began frantically making preparations for us all to return to the coast almost immediately upon our arrival in Greenville. Rudy and I knew that they were just beginning to remove the dead from the destruction and that there would be no electricity, no water, no food, no shelter, and no plumbing once we got home. Even with that knowledge, there was something inside of us that wanted to go home. We checked our values list to help us decide if we would be accompanying my mother and her elderly friend back into the devastated area. Our answer was there, at the very top of the list in values number one and two:

1. Keep the children safe, healthy, and happy.

2. Stay together no matter what.

When I explained to my mother that, for the sake of the children, we were not going to head to the coast with her, she was very upset with me. She also didn't understand why Rudy, who is the man of the family, was not going with her. Rudy and I learned a long time ago that if we stay together, everything works out for the best. We stayed together.

As my mom, Deb, and Miss Evelyn drove away with a trunk loaded down with gasoline in bleach bottles and kitty litter bottles, since they could not find any gas cans, we prayed that they would make it home safely and that when they got there, they would find what they were looking for—their homes. Rudy and I had everything we needed with us: our children, our commitment to each other, our love through thick or thin, and let's not forget, our cat. Everything else seemed so unimportant.

Six days passed before I spoke with my mother again and found out that her house was still standing, but had taken on over 25 feet of water from the massive tidal surge that Katrina had pushed ashore. Miss Evelyn's house had eight feet of water in it. My house was still standing, but had taken on waist-deep salt water and mud.

In the meantime, Rudy and I had work to do. Since we could not contact anyone we knew and cared about, and my mom had headed home, we were on our own. We studied the Atlas that we picked up at a gas station and decided to give Birmingham, Alabama a try. We made some phone calls, drove to a town we had never been to before, secured the last available apartment, and moved in on Sunday, eight days after we left home.

On Monday, September 5th, I led three teleclasses for Coach University. On Tuesday, I conducted client coaching calls. I know I could have canceled everything and taken the month off, but having a purpose bigger than survival proved to be an important part of our being able to get settled and back in the flow of life so quickly. Very high on our list of values is to do work that we love! The students that I had on my teleclasses in September and October of 2005 and my clients who all went through this with me were incredible. They will hold a special place in my heart for the rest of my life. I am filled with gratitude for them and continue to have relationships with them.

While on a visit to the Red Cross Shelter in Birmingham, we were approached by a wonderful woman, who has since become my friend, named Kristi McHale. Kristi, her husband Danny, two children, and their entire network of friends, family, and co-workers initially supplied us with blow-up mattresses and a TV. Within weeks they had nearly furnished our apartment. Kristi is my Katrina angel and I am so appreciative of her and her efforts to help my family recover.

We returned to Hattiesburg to retrieve Rudy's car and found Nancy and her family in the dark, without a phone, and having experienced the wrath of a Category 3 hurricane. Katrina was so big that it caused utter devastation hundreds of miles from the coastline.

Nancy told us an amazing story of how in the middle of the storm, she had a strong feeling to move Rudy's car. Under much protest from her husband and daughter, and not knowing how to drive a stick, Nancy went out in the middle of the storm, moved Rudy's car, and within an hour a huge tree fell right where it had been parked. You should have seen Rudy hug Nancy! It was a hug for the record books for sure.

Since the storm, there have been so many blessings, moments of synchronicity, and an outpouring of generosity from many people, including total strangers, that my story could go on forever. I am especially grateful to the coaching community for their outpouring of support in the form of cash, clothing, books, supplies, time, and energy. Since my entire family was affected, I really didn't have anyone to turn to for support. Every moment of every day was a blessing. I am so thankful to have a business that is totally portable and that I work with people all over the country and even internationally. Most of the people from my community and most of my family lost everything, including their jobs and businesses.

My mother and her five siblings are all without a home. My brother lost his home, which he took many years to renovate from a small bungalow to a huge family home in the Lakeview area of New Orleans. He had 12 feet of water in Katrina and eight feet in Rita. My stepsister lost her home in Pascagoula, Mississippi, 110 miles from New Orleans. My best friend Megan lost her historic beach front home in Bay Saint Louis. Both of Megan's sisters lost their homes. Eighty percent of the families where my kids attended school lost their homes. But worst of all, my uncle's wife lost her mother, who drowned in her home five miles from any body of water. The roof caved in, knocked her out, and she drowned in two feet of water.

Since moving back to Bay St. Louis is not an option for us, my family and I have moved from Birmingham to Pensacola, Florida. We are appreciative of all of the support and amazing friendships we established in Birmingham, but we are much more at home here. My kids are in school, doing well, but often speak of home. They both cry sometimes, especially when the holidays roll around. My son has been diagnosed with Post Traumatic Stress and is deep in the tunnel of that illness. He has had a hard time adjusting to being the new kid two times in the past year, especially considering he was in a class back home with seven kids. His close friends are still in touch via long phone conversations and a Yahoo group. Since moving to Pensacola in June of 2006, he is making new friends, doing better in school, and looking forward to high school next year. He has not touched his trumpet or his bass guitar since the storm.

Jolie is dancing on a highly competitive dance team with a great director. She loves her new school, new friends, and her new life. She misses her old friends, but since she was just eight when the storm hit, she is slowly forgetting her past.

I am in the midst of joining forces with Tammy, a woman originally from Biloxi, who lives in the San Francisco Bay Area. A total stranger that I met at a conference introduced us. Tammy's parents lost their home and in her efforts to help them, she started a non-profit agency called Adopt a Coast Family (www.adoptacoastfamily.org). I am working with her to identify more hard-working families that still need help to recover. Many people, especially home owners, have not received any money from their insurance or the government. They are struggling to survive. I will also be using my marketing skills to bring in more donations.

My dear friend Megan and her family are living on a boat in Destin, Florida. She just can't bring herself to invest her time, energy, and love into another house at the moment. Her loss has been profound and her healing is slow but steady and extremely hopeful. She is a bright, loving star that God has gifted the earth with. Before Katrina, we met every weekday morning for coffee and a workout. Now that I am in Pensacola, we meet in Navarre each Tuesday and Friday to work out together and visit. A 25-mile journey is a small price to pay to get a hug from my friend, my soul sister, my buddy. We now know that our friendship, our relationship, will survive anything. We both have hope of living within a few blocks of each other again in the future.

About half of the people in our lives have moved away to places like Colorado, Georgia, Alabama, New York, and even Canada. The other half of the people in our lives have stayed in the devastated area. I pray for them all every day as each group has their own struggles to contend with. For the people who left, there is a sense of disconnection from the community and the guilt of not being there to help rebuild. There is a deep sense of loss.

For the people who stayed in the community, it is the day–to-day struggle of surviving the Katrina Cough, the ramped staff infections, and the rat and mosquito infestations. It is the struggle to have to look at and be a part of the destruction and debris that is still everywhere. It is the struggle to rebuild their homes and businesses. It is the struggle to keep their children healthy and happy.

For all of us, it is a struggle to develop the "new normal" for our lives and to put the pieces back together. It is the struggle to rebuild our homes, businesses, and our sense of purpose. It is the struggle to find a way to make a living to pay the mortgages on the houses that no longer exist and that the insurance company will not pay for. It is the struggle to receive the grant money that has been slotted for us all, but no one that we know has received. It is a struggle for purpose, hope, and dignity.

Although many of us lost friends and family in the storm, those of us who remain still have each other. The relationships that we have are forever altered, but somehow hold a deeper meaning to all of us. There is so much love between us. There is so much love being sent to us. What an amazing adventure.

The Lessons of Hurricane Katrina

There have been many lessons and growth opportunities for me and mine in the wake of Katrina, some logistical, some emotional, some spiritual. I am going to share a few with you here that have been powerful.

Don't Rely on Cell Phones

I remember when I was younger, before we all had cell phones, if I was going on a trip, I would let my mother know the name and phone number of my destination. Today, we depend so heavily on our cell phones that no one really knows where we are going most of the time. When Katrina hit, not only did it take out the cell towers so that the people who were still in the hurricane zone could not use their phones, but it also took out the area codes 228, 504, and 985, making it impossible to call even outside of the area. You see, if a 228 cell phone is in Birmingham and is trying to call a number in Los Angeles, the call is routed through the 228 switch. So if the 228 switch is down, the call cannot be placed. Let your close family and closest friends know where you are going, so they can call you directly in case of an emergency.

KNOW YOUR VALUES AND WHAT IS MOST IMPORTANT TO YOU

I am not talking about the values that other people say you should have. I am talking about what it is that you truly value. The things in your life that you know are in line with who you are and what is important to you. Here are my top five values: Family, Fun, Authenticity, Prosperity, and Community. What are your top five values? Knowing your values allows you to confidently make decisions that are in line with the path that God has laid out for you. Your values are the deepest part of you, which is your connection to God.

ALLOW GOD'S BLESSINGS

One of the most difficult aspects of our Katrina Adventure has been allowing so many people to give us so many things, including their time, money, love, support, and things. You see, when you tend to be the one giving, receiving is not as simple as it sounds.

When my Katrina Angel Kristi approached me at the shelter and asked me if she could help us re-build our lives in Birmingham, at first I turned her down flat. I said, "We are so grateful for the offer, but we are very resourceful and we will be able to figure it all out just fine. Maybe you should help someone who really needs it."

Kristi, thank God, does not rattle easily, as she is a seasoned attorney and currently a stay-at-home mom, two very important jobs requiring advanced questioning and negotiation skills. She asked me the following list of questions:

"Was your home destroyed?"

"Yes, I think so," I replied, although I wasn't sure yet.

"Do you have family here to help you?"

"No," I replied.

"Do you have any place to stay?"

"Yes," I proudly replied. "We rented an apartment."

"Do you have any furnishings at all?"

"Well, no."

"Do you know anyone here in Birmingham?"

That's when I broke. It suddenly became clear to me that I did need help. We had lost my community of friends and family, many we would never see again. We had no support system and were alone. I knew in that moment that God had sent Kristi to me with her persistent self to be the catalyst for his work. Many tears were shed and Kristi got very busy on our behalf. Truck load after truck load, she and her husband Danny pulled up to our little apartment with clothes, shoes, food, furniture, kitchenware, etc., always delivered with a friendly smile and a ton of empathy, without one single ounce of pity.

This has by far been the biggest lesson for me and my husband so far. In order to receive God's blessings, we have to be able to allow God's blessings. Being strong, independent, and resilient are certainly wonderful character traits. However, when it comes to the abundance of gifts and happiness that God has for us, humility, humbleness, and acceptance are the orders of the day.

When You Have an Idea, Act on It

I am haunted by my plans. You know the plans I had that I was going to do as soon as I had time. Like take the kids floundering (fishing for flounder using a spear and a lantern under a full moon) like my uncle used to take me. I had plans to visit my neighbor, 92-year old Mrs. Necaise, who knew me before I was born, to bring her some lemon squares that she likes so much. I had plans to ride my bike with Megan from Cedar Point all the way to Clermont Harbor and take the whole day, stopping to eat at a beachfront restaurant called the Dock of the Bay. I had plans to bring a Thank You Card to the three sweet women who work at the Dollar Store for allowing Jolie and me to have a bake sale to raise money for Jolie's competition dance team to go to their national competition in San Antonio.

I had plans, a lot of plans.

Well, we never did take the kids floundering. My 92-year old neighbor had water up to her neck during the storm and has left town to stay with her sister in Colorado. I am sure I will never see her again. Cedar Point, Clermont Harbor, and The Dock of the Bay are all gone, having been wiped off the face of the earth by a 35-foot tidal surge. My daughter's dance team is not competing this year and will never be a team again, since most of the 45 girls on the team are scattered across the country, re-building their lives. As for the clerks at the Dollar Store, they are all victims of Katrina in the ultimate sense of the word. They died in the store trying to ride it out in what they thought was a safe place.

Stop planning and get out there. Stop thinking about picking up the phone and do it. Let the people you love know it. Let your gratitude for them be known in every moment. Because—as I am living proof—tomorrow you might not have the opportunity to say it to those you are thinking about.

CREATE A VISION FOR YOUR LIFE
THAT DOES NOT CENTER AROUND PLACES OR THINGS

Think bigger than that. What will the places and things that you attract into your life really bring you? Focus on that. Focus on the happiness of being in a place that you love, even if you are not there yet. Focus on the joy it is to be with the people you love and who love you, even when you are not with them. Focus on the wonderful feeling of peace you get being surrounded by your dream home and all of the wonderful things inside it. Happiness, joy, and peace are the real goals. Focus on what achieving them will really bring you.

Ask yourself these questions:
- Do I have an emergency plan in the case that my cell phone does not work?
- Do I know what my and my family's values really are and exactly what is most important to me?
- Am I able to receive the blessings that God wants to give me?

- What have I wanted to do in my area and in my life that I have not done?
- What neighbor or friend have I wanted to visit that I have not gotten around to?
- What vision do I have for my life, even if my life was turned upside down in a matter of hours?

I know this is some heavy stuff and some hard work, but trust me when I tell you that as stable as your life is right now, tomorrow could bring something entirely different. I am not suggesting that you live in fear—quite the opposite. Live with love, hope, and joy, because your life as you know it can change in an instant. Don't take any of it for granted—especially the relationships. Make your relationships deep and meaningful, vibrant and lasting, and live the biggest, fullest life you can live right now.

About
Jille Bartolome

Jille Bartolome, Master Certified Coach and Business and Life Coach specializes in partnering with entrepreneurs, business owners, and individuals to be more productive, profitable, and balanced in their professional and personal lives.

"My purpose is to guide others to find and achieve their purpose."

Jille acquired her Bachelor of Science degree in Behavioral Psychology from the University of Southern Mississippi. She is a graduate of CoachU, where she is currently on faculty. Jille has received the highest credential of Master Certified Coach through the International Coach Federation.

Before becoming a Coach, Jille owned an executive and high-tech placement firm. Her experience also includes Career Advising and High Level Corporate management. It seemed only natural for Jille to combine these experiences and skills with her gift in guiding others to help themselves, and in 1997 she began her coaching practice. Since then, people all over the United States, as well as internationally, have benefited from her " I coach, you win" approach.

Jille's latest endeavor is The Inner Beauty Institute (www.innerbeautyinstitute.com), where she is heading up the research and development of products and services that guide people toward utilizing their own inner power and wisdom.

Jille has earned a solid reputation as strategic coaching partner and has been called "The Velvet Hammer" by her students and clients due to her warm yet edgy approach to coaching.

For more information, email coachjille@humanedgeinc.com, call 228-466-9478, or visit www.humandegeinc.com.

Using Imagery to Enhance Relationships

By Jeanie Marshall

Images are powerful and enliven life! You can't buy them at the corner grocery store; you create them from within. They travel on, in, with, and through words, both of which are created by and reflect your consciousness, intention, and meaning.

As a writer, speaker, and frequent communicator, I love and rely heavily on words. There are many who believe that words are the key to communication. Yet words are only one aspect of relating to others. Images can be more creative than words or actions. However, when images, words, and actions align with each other, all are especially creative.

Fundamental as A, B, C

I have a model in mind whenever I talk with a client. The model involves two questions: Where are you now? Where do you want to be? Sometimes I ask these questions directly; sometimes I just listen and watch for images without asking questions. Everyone constantly transmits messages about both places.

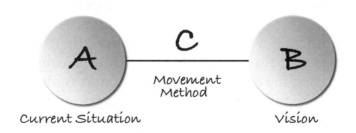

A: Current Situation. The place to start is where you are. Consider a shopping mall map. X marks where you stand. The current situation is the starting place, and remains the starting place if you continue to focus your attention here. While it can be cathartic to include evaluation and history, choose brevity rather than long-windedness when describing an uncomfortable situation if you expect to move from it. When the current situation is one you desire to recreate again and again, constant focus is beneficial.

B: Vision. The vision is where you desire to be (for example, the mall's book store, third level). Your work is to create a compelling vision. When you think about your life, of course, B is more than a map location. It's a place in consciousness, which includes your preferences, desires, dreams, goals. You create the most compelling visions using intentional imagery.

A and B Together. You carry with you both your current situation (A) and your vision (B). You see the world through either, depending on the focus of your attention. If you focus on and expect a dreadful interaction with your boss, you collude to create a dreadful experience. If you focus on and expect an empowering interaction, you create an empowering experience. You constantly create your relationships with your expectations and focus. The world responds to your emphasis of A or B.

C: Movement/Method. When you move from A to B, you use some method or path (C). Your focus of attention propels you. The method might be comprehensive or short-term, effective or haphazard. The path might be circuitous or direct, bumpy or smooth, obvious or obscure. You move in the direction you look.

Simple as A, B, C. I described the process in the most efficient and effective order: (1) succinct description of A plus (2) clarity of B reveals (3) options of C. The more compelling the vision, the more obvious the options to move and embrace B.

In an uncomfortable current situation, first recognize the discomfort and then intentionally focus in a more pleasant direction. Focusing constantly on the discomfort only creates more discomfort, because what you give your attention to, expands. So, recognize the discomfort and give it a name (for example, conversation with Ellen). With the current situation simply defined, you can more easily shift your attention to B by thinking and talking about your dreams, hopes, and expectations. The key is to make B more familiar than A.

"WOULD YOU TELL ME, PLEASE, WHICH WAY I OUGHT TO GO FROM HERE?"
"THAT DEPENDS A GOOD DEAL ON WHERE YOU WANT TO GET TO,"
SAID THE CAT.
"I DON'T MUCH CARE WHERE—" SAID ALICE.
"THEN IT DOESN'T MATTER WHICH WAY YOU GO," SAID THE CAT.
"—SO LONG AS I GET SOMEWHERE," ALICE ADDED AS AN EXPLANATION.
"OH, YOU'RE SURE TO DO THAT," SAID THE CAT.
"IF YOU ONLY WALK LONG ENOUGH."
~ LEWIS CARROLL, ALICE'S ADVENTURES IN WONDERLAND

The Alice Effect: A, C, B. Assume you're in a current painful or uncomfortable situation (A) with a person, place, thing, idea, or yourself. Truly, this uncomfortable current situation can move you (C). Swirling in a cesspool is movement; however, movement alone can't get you where you want to be without giving your attention to or toward B.

Compelling Vision. With a compelling vision to draw and inspire you, your path is more pleasurable, even with bumps and confusion. You'll move where you want to be if you point yourself toward B. You create the kind of relationships you want by giving your attention to the elements you appreciate in relationships.

When A and B are One. When you're clear about your vision, the Universe handles the methods and details, opening pathways for you to experience your vision as the current situation. Before or after you experience one vision, a new one emerges, keeping the process in continuous motion.

Images are a Natural Part of Life

Everything starts with your thoughts; all thoughts are accompanied by images, whether or not words or actions are involved. Images and thoughts are so interrelated that sometimes it's hard to distinguish them. Frankly, it's not necessary. Lump them together or separate them. The principles of creating relationships and all aspects of life are the same, whether you apply them to images, thoughts, words, or actions.

You have your own unique images, symbols, and impulses. Many are natural and spontaneous. Some images are splashes and flashes you may not fully comprehend. Others may be as clear as you see with your physical eyes. Some arrive in your nighttime dreaming, forgotten or remembered in the morning or days later. Others emerge through processes or techniques like goal setting, meditation, writing or reading poetry, or conversations with yourself or others. To become more aware of images that occur to you naturally, set an intention to notice them. Simply ask yourself, "What image relates to this specific idea or thought?" Or, "What image represents an empowering relationship with my friend?"

As you discover and work with techniques, don't give your power away to them. Let techniques help you find the power in you. A technique gives you a focus. Techniques are like bicycle training wheels. When bike riding feels natural, you remove the training wheels. When you embody the skill that's the purpose of the technique, you no longer need the technique. If continued use comforts you, don't abandon the technique. Just remember the power is in *you*.

Discover, identify, create, and play with images and techniques to focus your attention. Train yourself to direct and redirect your attention. Use imagery to sharpen or soften your focus, lift your consciousness, and enhance your relationships.

Re-frame a Situation for Empowering Change

An empowering image can re-frame a situation or be a comforting distraction from a difficult situation. For example, Brad told me about a behavior pattern he recently decided to change when relating to his boss. He denounced the old behavior, calling it "insane" and "silly." I suggested he re-frame and re-name that characterization to think of the old behavior as a "step," a viable way to manage himself in the past. He's changed, so his behavior must change.

With the "step image," Brad's shoulders immediately released tension. He saw himself on a stairway, moving upward. In his mind's eye, he began to create interesting stairways: colorful, spiral, or marble. His attitude continued to lift upward as he moved up his stairway, diverting himself from the specific, uncomfortable situation. When his attention returned to the relationship with his boss, he still felt empowered. When his empowerment waned, he had a meaningful image on which to refocus his attention.

The step image gave Brad a new way to see change in his life, an empowering way to integrate this specific change more fully, and a continuing process to integrate increasingly more empowering future changes. He'll always be changing—*always*. Now he has a series of steps, or stairs, to direct movement in more enjoyable ways. The steps/stairs might be with him for many years, or he might find other appropriate images.

All change requires movement. When you want to intentionally change some aspect of a relationship, start by recognizing the need for change. After practicing disempowerment for a while, the first glimmer of change is often met with clumsy awareness. With practice, you embrace empowerment more fully.

If your life is going exactly as you want, you needn't make intentional changes. Continue what you're doing; changes will occur naturally. However, if you feel disempowered in some aspect of your life, work intentionally with images to enhance momentum toward more satisfying experiences.

From Resentment to Appreciation with Imagery

Helen resented her boss's disempowering way of treating her. When she suggested white, Jake chose black; when she suggested black, he chose white. He found fault with projects that were 99% excellent, rarely alluding to the excellence.

Her expressed feelings pinpointed the starting place: guilt about her contempt for him and incompetence at creating a problematic relationship. She wanted to change the dynamics to be more satisfying.

As Helen spoke about Jake, I listened to her words and watched for images surrounding her thoughts. As her words expressed imagery (for example, black and white), she gave clues for effective imagery work with her. Using only black and white, we created gray by merging them. Gray in any shade isn't very vibrant, but thinking of white as the combination of all colors, and black as the absence of colors, we generated greater imagery. Colors became an integral part of Helen's imagery work.

Helen articulated another image, "feeling like he was hitting me over the head." This diminished her clear thinking, especially in Jake's presence. I asked what the object was. A hammer? A sponge? To her, it felt like a hardcover book. We worked with this image to divert her attention from Jake to a picture she could easily have power over in her mind's eye. She learned to identify and change the book.

We discussed the book's attributes. The title—what was it and could she change it? The size—how big was it and could she make it bigger or smaller? How does he hold the book—using one or both hands?

Once in the spirit of imagery, we imagined Helen sitting in Jake's office. One time, the book was Peter Drucker's *Management: Tasks, Responsibilities, Practices*. We envisioned Jake stop in midair before hitting her, taking the book in both hands, putting it on the desk, and finding the chapter, "Developing Management and Managers." We both tuned into this image and watched an enlightened expression change Jake's face. Then he closed the book, picked up her report, and gave careful, constructive feedback that was empowering to both. As we played with these images, I noticed Helen's face and head relax.

One day, Jake telephoned Helen while he vacationed at his Cape Cod cottage. He described the ocean breeze, his favorite drink, and the porch facing the beach. He was mellow, charming, and receptive to her ideas. In her mind's eye, she saw his setting. More importantly, she visualized how mellow he was. When tensions are particularly stressful, she imagines him at his cottage, mellow. Jake may or may not relax, but even if she just imagines him mellow and receptive, she relaxes.

All this imagery work is for Helen; it's not intended to manipulate Jake. As Helen imagines certain pictures of effective interactions, Jake is far more likely to step into her picture and participate with her. Interactions are co-creative. When Helen imagines upcoming interactions as empowering, the actual interactions are more empowering. Words and actions flow from images, thoughts, and expectations. Form follows thought.

The most potent images are ones the client articulates. Sometimes I suggest an image I think the client will relate to or, as with Brad, if a predominant image is so strong it blocks new ones. I don't force images on the client. I listen and look; I'm a witness and a guide.

Empowering Images for You

You see the world through your own eyes. Others' perspectives might be interesting, even enlightening, but your focus determines your experiences. As with a photograph or an oil painting, you and your friends can look at the same picture and see different perspectives, too many to articulate or agree on. While you may agree on the picture's general subject, if you look at the left corner and someone else at the right corner, you each see different images. All are valid.

You know when your images are empowering by how you feel. If you feel pleasant feelings and sensations, the images resonate with your visions and desires, and therefore are empowering. Unpleasant feelings and sensations mean the images don't resonate with your visions and desires, and are disempowering. You create your experiences in the direction of your curiosity, whether you feel good or not.

Natural and Intentional Imagery

Natural imagery is imagery you don't really think about or plan; it's familiar, practiced, or spontaneous. Intentional imagery is imagery you deliberately evoke for a purpose.

Here's an example of natural imagery: When you say, "I'm working at my computer," you naturally transmit images of work, attitudes about work, and elements of your environment. How strongly you associate with these images and the listener's receptivity determine the extent they're transmitted and received.

Here's an example of intentional imagery: You say, "I'm working at my computer" with an intention to assure your boss that you're confident about completing the project on schedule, so you imagine yourself triumphant and the project completed— packaged, bound, or delivered.

The words are the same in these examples. The intentions, attitudes, images, and meanings differ. Your vocal inflection helps convey meaning, but the images and attitudes most powerfully transfer the meaning.

Natural imagery happens all the time, with or without your awareness. Intentional imagery occurs with your forethought or effort. Both are important and work together. The process of creation works whether the images are positive or negative; whether they feel good or not; whether you're awake or asleep.

Your starting place is recognizing the images you currently transmit. What do you see, imagine, touch, taste, intuit, or hear inside you?

If you currently find yourself in uncomfortable situations, you're using negative images—naturally, intentionally, or in some combination. If you currently find yourself in desired situations, you're using positive images—naturally, intentionally, or in some combination. And, of course, you experience varied results with different mixes: natural, intentional, positive, negative, mild, strong.

The most effective communicators (trainers, actors, etc.) use overhead slides or props or demonstrations to maximize their effectiveness in combining visual and auditory components. I, too, advocate such techniques. However, the visual imagery I'm speaking about occurs in the energy field, not seen through physical eyes. That sight is inner sight; the process, imagination.

If you talk to a group about a tomato, everyone creates unique images of the tomato. If you elaborate with juicy words while you imagine a delicious, ripe, red tomato, your listeners' mouths might begin to water as mine is now. One may prefer a tomato right from the vine with a little basil, another imagines eating a succulent tomato in an arugula salad, another bites into a beefsteak tomato on a medium-rare hamburger on a bun with lettuce and pickle. And have you ever eaten a tomato with a squeeze of lime?

Everything you manifest on the physical plane is a process of co-creation. Sometimes you co-create what you like or prefer and sometimes you co-create what you don't like or prefer. Your creations depend on where you put your attention. If you give your attention to resentment, you're in a relationship with resentment, and so you co-create with resentment. If you give your attention to peace, you co-create with peace. You don't need to ask permission of the other (person, place, thing, or idea) to be a partner, just give your attention to the other, and you're in partnership.

WYSIWYG

WYSIWYG (phonetically Wizzy-Wig) is an acronym for What You See Is What You Get. The term became popular when Apple announced the first computer that displayed a screen that looked like a desktop: what you saw on screen was what you got in print. I apply that phrase to the idea of imagery, slightly expanding the words to clarify the meaning. What you see in your imagination is what you get in your life. What you draw in your inner vision, you draw into your experiences.

If you worry about a relationship with someone—dreading meeting in-laws or your boss's boss—you imagine not-wanted ideas and images. If your feelings of dread are peppered with images and expectations of fears or ridicule, the more likely you'll experience the very dynamic you worry about. When the images are truly graphic, you manifest the worried-about condition more quickly and more often. If your worries become topics of conversation, you energize your negative expectations further. This pattern creates a cycle: experience a difficult situation, think about and/or discuss the situation, experience a new difficult situation either with the same person or others, and so on. If you experience the cycle long and often enough, you must be intentional to break the pattern. The familiar and practiced responses continue to expand until you interrupt the cycle.

All this may sound like really bad news. But it's *good* news because if you want to change your experiences from what you don't want to what you *want*, you can change your images and expectations to create what you want and where you want to be. When changing a long-time habit of focusing on not-wanted ideas, it may take time being consistent with focusing on wanted ideas to experience consistent, desired results. Your creation may not have the exact details as the imagery, but the essence will be the same if you're consistent about focusing on the thoughts and images you want. And so, you must practice. The more fun you have practicing, the more likely you'll practice consistently. Consistency is key.

Tammy Takes Flight

Tammy once feared airplane travel. Most of her flights were problematic in some way: unusually bumpy, mechanical problems, cancelled flights, etc. Her travel stories were entertaining and sometimes hilarious. What she didn't understand was how her engaging images in her storytelling created more of the same experiences.

Since travel was, and still is, integral to her job, this dynamic impacted her job effectiveness, work and personal relationships, and health. She arrived at meetings frazzled, stories flowing from her lips as if rehearsed in the taxi ride from the airport. More attention was focused on Tammy's latest travel than on her job competence. Her relationship with travel polluted her other relationships.

I asked about her latest trip so I could hear her words and see the images. I knew she could improve her experiences. What a storyteller! She presented details of travel maladies that the best screenwriters would envy or admire. Her own screenplay played out in her travels, sprinkled with colors, fascinating shapes, and peppy dialogue. I helped her write a new screenplay, based on scenes she wanted to experience.

Using her images, I helped her create a more empowering story about her recent trip, energizing it to match the entertainment of her disempowering stories. Sometimes I suggest clients stop talking about their problems and shift their attention to different subjects; however, Tammy is a brilliant storyteller with an eager audience, so helping her tell stories in more empowering ways was the better strategy.

When clients first work with me, they rarely understand they're the creators of their own lives. I plant seeds to articulate this during moments of readiness. Rather than convince Tammy that by changing her storytelling she'd change her future travels, I suggested she explore telling her stories differently to feel better about the latest trip. I knew she'd trust my suggestions more if I related them to the present situation rather than future travels. She needed a direct experience of changing her focus and watching her travel improve. One thought at a time. One step at a time.

As Tammy and I worked with travel, we also worked with other situations in her life. All situations interrelate. Travel was the most dramatic and sometimes traumatic part of her life, but as Tammy began using intentional imagery before, during, and after travel, she more easily used intentional imagery in relationships with her boss, husband, and others.

Tammy now finds most of her travels extremely pleasant. More importantly, her colleagues are far more interested in her creative ideas than her travel. When she tells travel stories, she focuses on wonderful people and enjoyable experiences. On some flights she even meditates!

Trust Unlocks the Willingness to Explore

In my client sessions, trust is a key element. I don't demand my clients trust me; I help them trust themselves. They tap their self-trust when trying unfamiliar techniques. I match a technique with each client to resonate with special needs. Sometimes it's a tried-and-true technique; sometimes it's so fresh and uniquely for the person that I'm not aware of its fullness until later. As trust builds, I express increasingly more empowering ideas.

I encourage the client to take the next step toward empowerment, the one most accessible from the starting place. If I suggest a client take three steps in one leap, trust dissolves and the process loses effectiveness. One step at a time builds trust for the next step. As the client notices results in the present situation, the next step is natural. This is practicing. This is relationship building.

Blocks and the Perception of Blocks

People often believe blocks in their energy field prevent them from doing (or not doing) something. It's really the *belief* in the blocks that prevent them, not the blocks. I start where the client is and work with the blocks or beliefs enough to join with and understand their perceptions. I respect and help clients move from where they are to where they want to be.

An empowering relationship to a block can include blasting it into little pieces, walking around it, stepping over it, or changing it into a more appealing form. You can make it smaller and less imposing or bigger and more ominous. I find with undue attention on a block, the latter happens.

Sometimes people become such "block experts" that they can't focus on anything else. If someone blames another for a block, I recognize this is the person's perception, without expressing wrong-doing or self-blame. When the person is ready, responsibility for creating one's own life—including blocks—is a natural, empowering step.

If someone puts great certainty in a block, I honor that the person isn't ready to relinquish it. Ultimately, the most empowering approach is to place the attention elsewhere because the block, and even its perception, will diminish or disappear when it's not fed energy. In the meantime, I engage with my clients to make the block less disempowering.

I start with the client's description of the block and encourage increasingly more empowering images. For example, a brown glob that represented Jane's ineffective boss became a pink parakeet, sang for a while, and then flew away when she and her boss opened communications. David imagined his right knee, with debilitating pain that prevented his running, as an iron gear in need of oil, which he lubricated three times a day in two-minute visualizations. One week later he returned to light jogging, and later ran the Boston marathon.

These are examples of the clients' images, not mine. Each client is unique, so the images are as well. Just like everything in life, images change. Some images change naturally; some images change intentionally. By working with images that represent conditions, it's possible to move more quickly through relationship problems.

I was Jane's third coach for her troublesome six-year relationship with her boss. Our client sessions were filled with more strategies than pink parakeets, but she flew further and faster with that image than any other single strategy, because we stopped focusing directly on the troublesome relationship!

I knew David's knee pain had a long history, but if we had had conversations about that history, we'd have spent years unraveling the meaning, because for each discovery, there would be more to uncover. He wanted to run the marathon successfully; he wanted to run his consulting business more effectively. His "oiling the gear" visualization distracted him in just the right amount to accomplish both. Now, five years later, he continues running both marathons and a multi-million dollar consulting business.

Meditation is a Quiet Revolution

People are meditating on trains and planes, as they jog or hike, in their showers and gardens, and in the middle of a workday. Meditation quiets the mind, but doesn't really stop it because the mind is designed for thinking.

I define meditation broadly, more in terms of its essence than its form. Meditation is a state of consciousness rather than a function of time, place, activity, position, quietness, or stillness. Meditation calms you, focuses your attention, enhances your relationships, and helps you be more receptive to energy and imagery.

During a meditative experience, it's most advantageous to focus on a non-contradictory thought or subject. Examples are: a silently repeated mantra; a soothing sound (music, a constant or rhythmic noise, a voice in guided meditation); an interesting visual image, such as a Mandela or sphere. If you prefer open-eye meditation, focus on a burning candle, swaying tree, or grains of sand. If you prefer moving while meditating, focus on your footsteps or a rolling brook as you walk.

People relate differently to meditation. Some experience detached sensations or feelings of lightness; others experience euphoria; others lose consciousness and awaken to expanded consciousness. Some feel calm afterwards; others feel exhilarated. Some are more aware of their physical senses; others transcend their physical senses. Some fall asleep; some awaken. Meditation may be universal, yet it's still a highly personal experience.

Before, during, and after meditation are fertile times to work with intentional images. Some people open themselves to receiving empowering images in their meditative awareness; others focus on previously identified empowering images to lift their consciousness during meditation. Images give the mind a place to rest.

Create Your Relationships With Empowering Images

So, inspire yourself to be creative. Create images. If you perceive a challenge in your life, identify an image to represent the challenge, then describe attributes of the image such as texture, distance, size, color, shape. Change the image into whatever pleases you: let pink lollipops represent sweet love; let a waterfall remind you to be in the flow of life. Envision the back cover of the book you want to publish next year. See yourself and your boss eager to greet each other as friends. Imagine tension uncoiling between you and a neighbor, turning into a pleasant image. Make your images playful, realistic, silly, formal, surreal, impressionistic, or any quality you want.

What you see in your imagination, you manifest in your life. What you draw in your mind, you draw into your reality. WYSIWYG. Life is as fundamental as A, B, C.

About
Jeanie Marshall

As a Personal Development Coach, Jeanie helps people to find the power within themselves. She uses traditional resources and innovative approaches to help her clients move from where they are to where they want to be. She has a keen inner eye that assists her in perceiving the magnificence of her clients, even when they're telling disempowering stories.

One of her greatest gifts as a consultant and coach is to hold the vision of her clients' true desires until they're able to step into the vision. Her consultation sessions are playful, inspiring, and transformative. She says, "the most joyous part of my professional life is working one-on-one with clients, which is a partnership of co-creative, empowering ideas."

Jeanie has an M.S. in Organization Development from the American University and NTL Institute in Washington, DC. She directs all activities of her consulting firm, Marshall House in Santa Monica, California. She conducts private consultations by telephone for clients all over the world, appears as a guest on television and radio shows, and has produced more than 700 guided meditations on audio cassette tapes. She now makes guided meditations and guided visualizations available on CD albums and MP3 downloads.

For six years, she produced and hosted a local television show, "Return to Center." She has been actively involved in the human potential movement and organizational development since 1980.

Also a prolific writer, Jeanie has web sites and blogs that are frequented by her clients, as well as others in the Internet community. You can find her voice and writing at the following sites:

• She has offered the DailyAffirm Personal Transformation Process since 1994, which is available at www.dailyaffirm.com.

• The Voice of Jeanie Marshall at www.jmvoice.com makes available her CD and MP3 albums.

• Writing for and by Coaches, at www.WritingByCoaches.com, offers writing resources for coaches and consultants to share their knowledge, wisdom, and experiences.

• JMviews Guided Meditation and Empowerment Consulting, online at www.JMviews.com, is a blog with writings about her philosophy.

For more information, visit any of these sites or Marshall House at www.mhmail.com or contact Jeanie at (310) 392-1987 or mhmail@earthlink.net.

The Ebb and Flow of Friendships: Knowing When to Let Go and Grow with Change

By Deb Yeagle

"THERE CAN BE NO FRIENDSHIP WHEN THERE IS NO FREEDOM. FRIENDSHIP LOVES THE FREE AIR, AND WILL NOT BE FENCED UP IN STRAIGHT AND NARROW ENCLOSURES." ~ WILLIAM PENN

Kelly and Nicole had been best friends since kindergarten. They grew up together through elementary school, survived their teenaged years, and continued to be inseparable during high school. As they went their separate ways to college, they vowed to keep in touch and be friends forever.

During the first couple of years of college, they stayed in touch through regular e-mails and reunited during holiday and summer breaks. As college graduation approached, their contact diminished to occasional run-ins during brief visits home from school, despite Kelly's repeated attempts to reconnect with her best friend. Kelly was crushed that her e-mails to Nicole went unanswered and her phone calls to Nicole's voice mail went unreturned.

Kelly and Nicole's friendship fell victim to geographical separation. Even though today's technological advances in communication through cell phones, the Internet, and e-mail have seemingly eliminated the physical distance between friends, these increased methods of communication don't necessarily substitute for the emotional intimacy needed to sustain a close relationship.

Geography, however, was not the main reason that Kelly and Nicole grew apart. Their friendship also ebbed as Nicole experienced personal changes in her life. As she grew into adulthood during her college years, her values changed. She developed new friendships in college as she gravitated toward other people with similar ideals and beliefs. Kelly had trouble accepting one of the hard facts of life: people change.

Friendships that are formed during adult years can also be impacted by changes. While adults also experience personal changes through individual growth, other types of changes that occur during adult life are more likely to affect friendships. New demands on time due to marriage, parenthood, work obligations, family or personal health problems, or different interests and hobbies are the typical reasons why old friendships die and new friendships are born.

Derrick and Ethan met in college and became fast friends. They joined the same fraternity and partied for five years at school before graduating with their degrees in accounting. They both joined the same firm after school and shared an apartment in the real world. Their party lifestyle continued as they settled into their new jobs. After the first few months, Derrick noticed Ethan beginning to take his work more seriously. When Derrick left work for happy hour, Ethan remained at the office. Each began to travel in different circles. The two friends who had been as close as brothers began to drift apart.

Kim and Lisa met when they became neighbors. They were both stay-at-home mothers with two young children who were the same age. Raising their children and working hard as homemakers, Kim and Lisa bonded and became best friends. When their children entered school, Kim grew restless at home and decided to go back to work. Lisa became more involved with her kids, volunteering at their school, coaching her son's soccer team, and serving as her daughter's Girl Scout troop leader. Even though Kim and Lisa did not have as much in common as they did when they first became friends, they remained committed to keeping their friendship alive.

Lasting friendships are one of life's most treasured relationships. Yet lifelong friendships are rare. How do you survive the emotional letdown of losing a friend? How do you know when it's time to let go of a friendship? What can you do to grow with the changes in your friendships? What can you do to maintain and nurture long lasting friendships?

Getting from Sadness to Gladness

"So plant your own garden and decorate your own soul, instead of waiting for someone to bring you flowers." ~ Anonymous

When Kelly graduated from college, she felt a temporary heartache since Nicole was not there to celebrate with her. Kelly had made her own friends in college, but she still missed her best friend. She was having trouble overcoming the loss of Nicole's friendship. Her emotional frame of mind was even more unsettled since she was anxious about entering into the working world. A few days before leaving home for her new job, she shared her despair with her Mom.

"Kelly, do you remember how it felt when your Aunt Samantha passed away?" her Mom asked. Kelly reflected on the loss of her aunt, considered by Kelly as more of a friend, who passed away when Kelly was in high school.

Kelly recalled the sadness as she fondly remembered her aunt, and replied "Of course I do, Mom. I was devastated."

"Right, but when she passed away, you allowed yourself to grieve, and once we mourned your aunt, you were able to accept her death. Nicole has not passed away, but you have lost her as a friend, and you have not allowed yourself to grieve. It's bottled up inside you and that's why you're having so much trouble accepting the end of your friendship."

Kelly considered her Mom's point and listened to her advice. "Allow yourself to be sad. Cry, or do whatever it takes to let out your feelings. Eventually you will find that thoughts of Nicole will generate memories of the good times together instead of sadness." Kelly fell into her Mom's arms and sobbed as she released the feelings of loss that had been pent up for years.

Anyone who has ever experienced the loss of a friendship knows the feeling is similar to the grief experienced when you've lost a loved one through death. An important first step in surviving the loss of a friendship is to allow yourself to grieve for your old friend.

Once past the grieving process, it's critical to avoid blaming yourself for the death of a friendship. "Kelly," Mom continued as she sensed Kelly's sobs slowing down, "It's not your fault that Nicky changed. People change for their own reasons that have nothing to do with you."

Everything happens for a reason, even though those reasons may not be apparent to you. You should expect people to change, and expect these inevitable changes to have impacts on friendships. Accepting those changes will help you to deal more effectively with them.

As Kelly loaded the final few boxes into her car and prepared to leave home for her new apartment, her Mom's heart began aching. She knew she'd have some grieving of her own to do when Kelly left her room at home for the last time. But before Kelly left she passed on one last piece of motherly advice. "Kelly, I'll miss you terribly, but I know you'll be fine on your own, succeed in your new job, and make new friends at work. I'm proud of you." Kelly's Mom struggled to maintain her composure as she continued. "But don't forget to see life as it is. Don't hold yourself captive to a vision of how it ought to be. Make the most of everyday by celebrating the little things. Have fun by finding something to laugh at and rediscover your sense of humor. It's much easier to learn to love what you have instead of always longing for what you're missing, or what you imagine you're missing. It's so much more peaceful."

Although her Mom did not specifically mention her friendship with Nicole, Kelly knew exactly what her Mom was talking about. Kelly realized that she'd be moving on with her life without her forever friend, and she'd survive. She'd not only survive, she'd thrive through relationships with new friends. Eventually, Kelly reached the point of accepting the loss of Nicole, occasionally reminisced about their good times together, and every now and then, sent Nicole an e-mail without caring if it went unanswered.

Letting Go

"SOMETIMES YOU HAVE TO LET GO TO SEE IF
THERE WAS ANYTHING WORTH HOLDING ON TO." ~ ANONYMOUS

Sometimes letting go of a friendship is not by choice, as in Kelly's case, when she finally realized her friendship with Nicole could not be revived due to the personal changes in Nicole's life. But there are other times when you have to deliberately end a friendship.

Consider Derrick and Ethan's friendship. From Derrick's perspective, Ethan's interests and priorities changed. He spent more time at work than he did on the social scene. The basis for their friendship was Derrick and Ethan's common interests of working hard, partying harder.

From Elliott's perspective, Derrick still acted like he was in college. Elliott believed Derrick's shady work ethic was putting him in danger of losing his job. Elliott noticed Derrick taking long lunches during the day and sometimes returning reeking of alcohol, if he returned at all. Their different perspectives came to a head one Friday afternoon.

"Happy hour starts in 30 minutes, buddy!" Derrick said as he stopped in Elliott's office.

"I've got a deadline for this client that I need to meet early next week, so you go on without me and I'll see you at home later tonight," replied Elliott.

"What's wrong with you, man?" Derrick screamed. "You're such a stick in the mud, lately. You're boring and you're acting like an old man! Work, work, work, that's all you do anymore. What happened to Ethan the party animal?"

Ethan was insulted. "Derrick, when are you going to grow up? We've both got a job here. You can't go through the motions during the day, party all afternoon and into the night, and expect to keep your job. I still like to have fun, but not at the expense of my job!"

"You have no right to criticize my work. I work hard when I need to so I can party when I want to," Derrick shot back.

Conceding, and not wanting to anger Ethan further in case he needed his services as a designated driver later that night, Derrick walked out, saying, "Nevermind. Call me later if you want to hook up with us."

Ethan was frustrated because he knew Derrick didn't get it. He wasn't listening to Ethan's viewpoint and he didn't see what damage he was doing to his career. As much as he was concerned about Derrick, he knew that their friendship was slipping away.

Ethan also knew he had to stay true to himself. He could not compromise his work ethic or sacrifice his job for a friend who was influencing him to stray from his values and beliefs. Like Kelly, who remained true to her values when her best friend Nicole's values changed, Ethan had to decide between staying true to himself or to his best friend Derrick. He decided to move in with another accountant at the firm who shared similar interests and work hours. Even though he and Derrick were not as close as they had been in the past, Ethan made a committed effort to keep in touch with him on a regular basis.

There are other instances of having to purposely bring a friendship to an end. Besides friends whose values are inconsistent with yours, there are friends who violate the trust that forms the basis of the friendship. When your friend reveals a secret that you've entrusted to her, then the friendship is jeopardized. What your friend did is not right, but it's important to forgive and forget. Just like Kelly could not move forward because of pent up grief, you won't be able to take advantage of potential new friendships if you don't let go of past wrongdoings by former friends.

When you know what is right and listen to your inner voice, then you will know when it's time to let go of a friendship.

Growing with the Changes

"Look at people; recognize them; accept them as they are, without wanting to change them." ~ Helen Beginton

Kelly, Nicole, Derrick, and Ethan were not able to grow with the changes in their friendships. Kelly and Ethan remained true to themselves and went their separate ways from Nicole and

Derrick. Kelly learned how to survive the emotional letdown of the loss of her best friend, and Ethan learned how to let go of the friendship.

But not all friendships end due to personal changes. Kim and Lisa were close friends up to the point that their children began school. When they started going in different directions with their lives, Kim and Lisa did not grow apart. Instead, they accepted the changes that each other were going through. This acceptance was not immediate, however, and both Kim and Lisa had to learn how to make adjustments in their friendship so that it would truly grow with the changes.

Without criticizing, condemning, or complaining, Lisa initially supported Kim's decision to return to the working world, even though she knew she wouldn't be able to spend as much time with Kim as she used to. A few weeks after Kim returned to work, Lisa called Kim and asked her if she wanted to have a girls' night out sometime over the weekend. "I'm sorry Lis, I can't. I've got to attend a cocktail party with some clients on Friday night, and I promised Tom I'd go out to dinner with him on Saturday night since we hardly get to see each other anymore." Kim continued without taking a breath, "In fact, I'm glad you called because we still haven't gotten a babysitter for Saturday and I was wondering if you would mind watching the kids?" Lisa was speechless and hurt, but she agreed to keep Lisa and Tom's kids on Saturday. She had been trying to get together with Kim for weeks and she kept getting blown off.

Lisa began to feel insecure in the friendship. She started to feel inferior to her "working mother" friend and her self-confidence began to drop. Lisa also began to withdraw. She had made many attempts to keep in touch with Kim and didn't feel that Kim's level of commitment to the friendship was mutual, so she stopped trying to maintain contact with Kim altogether. Just as Lisa had almost completely given up on their friendship, Kim showed up at the door one evening out of the blue. "Hey, what's up? Where have you been?" Kim asked innocently. Lisa broke into tears. "What's wrong, Lis? What happened?"

Kim walked in and pulled Lisa over to the sofa and sat down with her. "What's wrong?" Kim repeated. "Are the kids OK? Did you and Steve have a fight? What's going on?"

Lisa was disturbed that Kim didn't even realize she was upset because of their dying friendship. She lashed out. "What are you doing here? I thought you had forgotten about me! Why aren't you at work?" Lisa cried.

Kim gave Lisa a hug and apologized. "That's why I'm here. I realize I've been neglecting you and our friendship. But don't read too much into things. I haven't been ignoring you. I've been busy. I still need you. I'm still your best friend. It's been hard for me to break into the working world. I've put all my time into this new job, and what's leftover I've given to Tom and the kids. I know it's been awhile since we've talked, but I miss you. I feel good about where I am in this new job, and I just came over to tell you I will have more time this week if you'd like to get together and get caught up."

Lisa was so relieved to hear these words from Kim. She assumed she had no value to Kim as a friend after repeated attempts on her part to maintain their friendship.

What could Lisa have done differently to avoid these feelings of rejection, insecurity, and inferiority? Instead of withdrawing, Lisa could begin by lowering her expectations. While both Lisa and Kim's personal changes were significant, Kim's changes placed more demands on her time and energy; Lisa's changes didn't add three hours of commuting time to her daily schedule and were not too far removed from her comfort zone as homemaker and mother. To help Kim grow with those changes, and to keep the friendship alive, Lisa could have been more sensitive to Kim's needs, being on the lookout for opportunities to help, instead of withdrawing. For example, Lisa could have called Kim to offer to help get her kids to and from school instead of calling to see when she could claim some of Kim's time to go on a girls' night out.

Lisa wasn't the only one who needed to make some adjustments. Once Kim settled into her new job, and Lisa and Kim began to renew their friendship, Kim began to consume a lot of Lisa's time complaining to her about so-and-so or the latest reorganization at work, and calling at all hours of the night to moan and groan about her job. At first Lisa felt pressure to help Kim, even though she couldn't relate to anything Kim was complaining about. Each time they got together, the conversation centered on Kim's problems at work. It was all about Kim, and she was becoming a high maintenance friend to Lisa. Kim was draining Lisa's energy to the point Lisa dreaded having to talk to Kim and hear the same old, tired story about how her life at work was doomed.

Lisa knew that she couldn't control Kim's happiness at work, she could only control her reactions to Kim's ranting and raving about problems with her job. So the next time Kim called Lisa to began her incessant venting, Lisa gave her the silent treatment. She laid the receiver down on the table much like her husband did when telemarketers called the house. After a few minutes, Lisa picked up the phone. Kim was still talking. Lisa tried to get Kim's attention. "Kim, KIM, KIM!!!!!"

The silence on the other end of the phone was stunning. Lisa had gotten Kim's attention. "Do you realize I have not been listening to you this entire time?" Lisa revealed. "I'm sorry you're not enjoying work right now, but it's consuming our conversations lately. Do you realize that?"

Kim was silent, realizing the imbalance of time spent with Lisa complaining about her problems and not enjoying each others' company or giving Lisa a chance to vent about uninspired school staff, rude soccer parents, and lazy Girl Scouts.

As Lisa and Kim became tuned in to each others' needs given the changes being experienced in their personal lives, they adjusted their friendship to avoid letting insecurities or high maintenance tendencies creep in.

Friendships can grow with changes when friends can accept personal changes in each other. Friends who remain committed to communicating with one another will find it easy to adjust as needed and keep the friendship alive.

Keeping in Touch

"FRIENDSHIP IS LIKE MONEY, EASIER MADE THAN KEPT."
~ SAMUEL BUTLER

As Lisa and Kim learned, despite the changes in their individual lives, friendships grow by keeping in touch. Their friendship survived some major life changes because each friend practiced the fundamentals of keeping in touch.

1. **Empathy.** Simply caring; treating friends with respect; staying in tune with your friends' needs; looking for opportunities to listen, comfort, and help; and letting them know they are important to you is the basis for nurturing friendships.

2. **Trust.** Relationships with your friends based on mutual trust pave the way toward long lasting friendships.

3. **Give and take.** Time is the best thing you can give a friend, not money or material things. A friend should ask for your time, not your money. When a friend gives you her time, then show your appreciation and return the gift.

4. **Commitment.** It's not enough to be concerned, you need to be committed. Loyalty and devotion to your friends is the highest form of commitment.

5. **Communication.** It's a two way street. If you abuse it, you become high maintenance. If you blow it off, you risk losing touch with your friend.

Once Kelly learned to grieve the loss of her best friend Nicole, and accepted the changes in her personal life, she carried out her commitment to keep in touch with Nicky. Even though Ethan's work ethic differed drastically from Derrick's, he remained concerned about his former best friend's future and was loyal to him. By keeping in touch, Kelly and Ethan made a committed effort to maintain their friendships with Nicole and Derrick.

When Kelly received word from her Mom that her high school class was having their five year reunion during the upcoming summer, she reluctantly decided to attend. Kelly was more interested in the opportunity to visit with her Mom than she was in reuniting with high school classmates.

Kelly arrived at the reunion without any expectations. She imagined only a few of her high school classmates would attend. She ordered a drink and reunited with a few of her teammates from the field hockey team. After getting caught up on the gossip about some of the most popular graduates from her class, she returned to the bar for another drink. As she placed her order with the bartender, she felt someone touch her on the shoulder. Turning around, she felt her heart stop and her jaw drop. Nicole stood there smiling and embraced her with a warm, heartfelt hug.

"Oh, my God!" cried Kelly. "I didn't expect to ever see you again."

Nicky was apologetic. "I'm so sorry, Kel. I'm so glad you didn't give up on me. I've lost my way and I'm looking for an old friend to help me find myself again." Kelly and Nicole spent the entire evening getting caught up with each other. Kelly was shocked to hear how Nicky had crossed the line into dangerous territory. She cringed when she learned about Nicky's dependence on drugs. She sympathized when she realized Nicole had been recruited into the wrong crowd at college. In turn, Nicky was saddened when she realized how badly she had hurt Kelly. Both Nicole and Kelly were glad that Kelly had maintained contact with Nicole, even though it was only one-way communication for many years. Keeping in touch allowed two best friends to reunite, reconnect, and eventually renew their relationship.

Ethan had advanced in the accounting firm and was lead accountant for a client that required forensic accounting support. He needed someone with an accounting background who also had the ability and personality to investigate potential criminal matters related to the account. As Ethan began to accept the differences between himself and Derrick, he appreciated Derrick's accounting skills, but also understood that Derrick did not have the personality that was content to sit behind a desk all day. Keeping in touch with Derrick allowed Ethan to learn more about Derrick's strengths and weaknesses at work.

When Ethan approached Derrick about the forensic accountant job, Derrick was cautious at first. He assumed that Ethan would require long work hours with little or no downtime to settle this account. Derrick hesitantly decided to talk to Ethan about the job. Ethan clearly explained his expectations about the investigative work to be conducted, and negotiated a deadline with Derrick.

Derrick was amazed at Ethan's flexibility with the work schedule. Through their renewed relationship at work, thanks to Ethan's commitment to remain in touch with Derrick, two best friends mended their relationship and began to spend more time together both at work and at the party scene.

While keeping in touch allows friendships to grow with the changes, this commitment to maintaining contact with friends is also critical to nurturing long lasting friendships. Other secrets to preserving long lasting friendships include not feeling guilty when it's difficult to keep in touch, and planning regular social outings.

With the passage of time, if it becomes difficult to maintain contact, then feeling guilty about not keeping in touch shouldn't prevent friends from reconnecting. Relationships with friends that are free of guilt can be easily renewed. If it's been awhile since you've called or e-mailed your friend, feeling bad about not keeping in touch shouldn't get in the way of re-establishing contact.

Regularly socializing with friends is as important to the relationship as providing help and encouragement to friends when needed. Sharing a meal or even going on vacations together brings friends closer and builds strong bonds that lead to long lasting friendships.

Some of the longest lasting friendships are similar to sibling relationships. Just like family ties, relationships with close friends are strong enough to last a lifetime.

The Vibrancy of Long Lasting Friendships

One of life's sweetest gifts is the love and companionship of close friends. Through the ebb and flow of life, relationships with friends provide support and comfort along the way. Sometimes, a friendship experiences its own ebb and flow. During times of personal and life changes, a friendship can suffer and even end unexpectedly. Accepting those changes and growing with them can keep the friendship alive, but sometimes it becomes necessary to let go of a friendship. Although it is one of life's most difficult decisions to make, when forced to choose between a friend and your principles, or when your trust has been violated by a friend, it's time to let go of the friendship, move on with life, and find new friends. Once you learn when to let go and how to grow with the changes, it becomes easier to manage your emotions when friendships wither.

Friendships require empathy, trust, give and take, commitment, and communication. While it may seem like maintaining and nurturing friendships requires considerable effort, like any vibrant relationship, the best friendships are **effortless** to sustain when both people are committed maintaining the connection.

About
Deb Yeagle

Deb Yeagle found her passion in life as a personal coach, doing business as "Coach Deb." As a life and career coach, Deb helps others succeed in their personal and professional lives. Her coaching program includes an action-oriented approach to help clients achieve their goals and solve their problems. Through assessment, goal-setting activities, action planning, and moral support, Deb's personal coaching services ensure results in personal and professional development. Deb's goal with all her clients is to help them reach their full potential…to learn…to love…to laugh…and to *live*.

During the course of her coaching practice, Deb has published numerous articles on various topics including achieving life-work balance; curing workaholics; establishing effective time management habits; dealing with change; resolving conflict; avoiding communication breakdowns; and eliminating boring, monotonous routines.

Deb graduated from James Madison University (JMU) in Harrisonburg, Virginia, with a Bachelor of Science degree in Computer Science. She began her employment with the Federal Government in 1981 as a high school student apprentice, worked her way through college as a cooperative education student, and began a career in software and database development after graduation from JMU. She has over 13 years of experience in supervisory leadership, through which she gained practical experience in professional and personal coaching.

For more information, visit www.coachdeb.net. To contact Deb, call (540) 907-6789 or e-mail coachdeb@comcast.net.

Back From Betrayal

By Penny R Tupy

"...FOR EACH HUMAN ACTION CONNECTS AND CHANGES AND AFFECTS, DYNAMICALLY, MANY BILLIONS OF MINUTE PARTICLES—AND MANY MILLIONS OF LARGER PARTICLES—AND MANY THOUSANDS OF PARTICLES THE SIZE OF PEOPLE. WE ARE CONNECTED IN WAYS SO PROFOUND THAT NO ONE HUMAN CAN EVER HOPE TO UNDERSTAND THEM ALL. AND YET ON EVERY LEVEL, IN EVERY WAY WE HAVE EVER FOUND TO LOOK OR MEASURE OR INVESTIGATE, THE CONNECTION SIMPLY GROWS MORE PROFOUND.
I AND THOU—WE ARE ONE."
~ JOANNA BARE – PHYSICIST, POET, COACH

Lisa sat at a nondescript table near the window and the front door of the busy truck stop just off the freeway. There was nothing to distinguish the place from any other small town truck stop except that to her it was home. Or, perhaps, memories of home would be a better description. Tears slid down her face leaving wet tracks in what was left of her make up. A box of tissues rested next to her on the table. Several were crumpled in her fists.

"I know I can't undo what I did. The harm to the kids, to you, to his family, his kids, her...."

A long pause ensued as fresh tears welled up and spilled out of the corners of her eyes. She took a shaky breath and swallowed hard.

Betrayal, especially within close relationships, is a wound that heals slowly. Betrayal comes in all shapes and sizes. There are the "smaller" betrayals of confidences not kept, gossip, or career sabotage. And there are the life-altering betrayals of incest, abuse, addictive acting out, or other momentous events. And there are betrayals that fall somewhere in between those two ends of the spectrum.

Betrayal leaves behind wounds that cut to the soul. The word itself is harsh to the ear and grates on the heart. Entire libraries of research, studies, and self-help books provide information, advice, and hope for working through the process of moving past betrayal and back to peace. Entire forests of trees have become the paper for articles and books telling us whether we should attempt to rebuild broken trust when someone has betrayed us and, if so, how to do it.

But what if we are the betrayer and not the betrayed?

Adam stepped up to the altar on a day set to honor the dead. Others before him, taking their turns, spoke the names of parents, grandparents, friends, and loved ones gone before. Shaky voices, ragged breaths, and the surreptitious wiping of tears told the story of loss behind the simple speaking of names.

But it was not a friend or loved one whose name Adam spoke as he stood before the altar in the prison chapel. It was the name of a stranger; a stranger killed by Adam's own hand. Barely whispered and heard only by a few, still the grief and pain, the shame and horror, howled on the breath of that whispered name.

How do we heal if we are the betrayer? So much is written for those who are harmed. Hearts are softened, arms are opened, and resources of all sorts are made available. But little is offered for the perpetrator of harm. It's easy to turn our backs on wrongdoers. It makes us uncomfortable, squeamish even, to knowingly be in the presence of someone who has wronged another. And yet... who among us has not? I sometimes wonder if our discomfort or squeamishness has more to do with our unwillingness to recall our own acts of betrayal than it does with the acts of another.

Twelve step groups for addicts have a very systematic healing approach for the betrayer. In Step 8, members make exhaustive lists of ways they have harmed others, then in Step 9, purposefully work to make amends. State correctional departments offer opportunities for inmates to apologize and collaborate with victims in healing through Restorative Justice programs. Most of us, though, are neither addicts nor criminals; we're ordinary human beings living perfectly human lives. Lives that include instances of betrayal or harm of those we love.

Amber was an average wife and mother. She loved her kids, she loved her husband, and she struggled with the everyday ups and downs of life in a family. When her husband had an affair and then regretted it, she worked to forgive him and to move forward. When he had a second affair, she battled her own rage and terror to keep the family together for the children. But when he left her a third time, she gave up. Reaching out to others for support, she met a man who was kind, gentle, and caring.

Amber fell in love and began an affair of her own. Eventually she left her husband for her new love. And, she left her children, both who were in their teens and who couldn't understand the chaos of the adult decisions swirling around them. Amber moved far away and only saw her children at holidays. Years later she is consumed with guilt and shame, but when she tries to talk to her friends or family to process her regret, they tell her she shouldn't feel that way.

Lisa, Adam, and Amber are all seeking some way to heal their internal pain resulting from their own actions. The first step of that process is acknowledgment of the pain caused to another. This is empathy. Compassion. It is moving beyond our own inner self-obsession to a place where we recognize and connect with the pain of another.

Betrayal healing begins with recognizing and admitting what we've done; it moves forward when we are heard. In Twelve Step groups, this is also very structured. After a member makes the list of wrongs committed—in Step 4—it is shared with another member—in Step 5—who will validate those wrongs and the pain caused to all involved. Validation is the necessary interface between admittance and atonement.

When Amber tried to talk to her friends or family about her remorse, she was invalidated. Instead of acknowledging her feelings of guilt in a way that would create space for her to move forward, they helped her stay stuck by telling her she shouldn't feel that way. Worse, they reminded her of her former husband's transgressions as a way of justifying her actions. Instead of feeling better, Amber only felt worse and her sense of disconnect from her children grew. Her healing got derailed.

Lisa had a better experience. As she sat with her former husband at that truck stop, soggy tissues crumpled in her hand, he allowed her to speak her regret and shame without interrupting. When she finished, he thanked her for being courageous enough to initiate the conversation and for her apology. Lisa began to move with a lighter heart beyond the torturous self-absorption with her own pain and toward making amends.

Adam's expression of remorse was never directly acknowledged. However, the ceremonial honoring of the dead where he expressed his wrongdoing was accepting and validating in its design. Personal one-on-one interaction is preferred. When it's not possible, a format of acceptance and understanding can be helpful and healing.

Looking at our wrongdoings with clarity and without excuses is the first step in betrayal healing. Moving beyond the quagmire of guilt and shame and toward empathy for those we've harmed is an integral part of that. Friends, family, or professionals in appropriate service fields do a great service when they can calmly hear and validate our process without downplaying our experience and without judgment. This is the foundation for healing.

Facing our misdeeds and being heard is often followed by an enormous sense of release and relief. Lisa felt as if the world had been lifted from her shoulders as she drove away from the meeting with her ex. Without accompanying actions, though, this sense of lightness is only transitory. The real work of betrayal healing is in making amends.

We can't change the past. It's tempting, sometimes, to wish that we could and some of us get stuck in reliving a fantasy of what we should have done—or could have done—or would have done if only we'd known. But we can't. The past is behind us—locked and unchanging. As obvious as it may seem, this means making amends can only be about the present and the future. And that means we need to turn our focus from what we've done to what we are doing and what we are going to do.

Making amends is most healing for the betrayer when they can directly impact, in a positive way, the present and future of those they have harmed. Step 9 tells addicts to make direct amends to people wherever possible, except when to do so would injure others.

Lisa, with her newfound energy and lightness, jumped right in making a list of people and corresponding actions. At the top of the list was fostering a better co-parenting relationship with her ex, closely followed by helping their children with life events neglected during the years of adversarial chilliness. She began to involve her former husband more in conversations regarding the children's needs and activities. As the girls saw their parents interacting cooperatively, a space opened where they were energized to move forward with their lives. Working together without old baggage weighing then down, Lisa and her ex-husband enticed their older daughters away from dead-end pursuits and they both enrolled in college.

Amends, like betrayals, come in all shapes and sizes. Sometimes, many times, a simple "I'm sorry, I was wrong," is all that's needed for all involved to heal and move forward. And then there are times when more is needed to repair our own sense of integrity and to heal. Once in a while, great betrayals require greater efforts at making amends. And sometimes, no matter what we do we can only heal our inner selves and understand that the relationship is beyond repair.

What if we cannot make direct amends for one reason or another? This is most often the case when the relationship, whatever its nature, cannot be restored.

Adam is limited by the state's rules regarding restorative justice. Although he can write a letter of apology to be read by his victim's family and the opportunity exists to interact with victims or their families to express regret or share information, those things are solely at the discretion of the victim or the victims' families. Adam has no ability to make that happen on his own. He is not empowered to make direct amends. Instead he must make amends by making positive contributions in a less specific manner. Adam was instrumental in starting a religious study group in the prison where he is incarcerated. He serves as a mentor within that group. Adam encourages other inmates to examine their choices and behaviors and to make better choices in all aspects of their lives.

Both Lisa and Adam report experiencing less inner turmoil, decreased shame, and increased inner peace and groundedness. They experience a sense of connection to their inner worth and to the world around them. Lisa feels greater satisfaction with her ability to make positive change; Adam is more motivated to seek creative ways to contribute constructively. Amber remains stuck. Without the validation she seeks, she experiences obsessive self-loathing alternating with denial. Her interaction with others tends to be an awkward dance of clinginess and withdrawal. Unable to move beyond her pained self-absorption, Amber cannot make amends.

The process for betrayal healing is straightforward and simple:

- Face our wrongdoings without rationalizations or excuses
- Acknowledge the harm we have done
- Move from internal obsession to empathy for those we've harmed—see it from their point of view
- Become vulnerable as we share our wrongdoing with another who will validate our experience
- Make amends by creating a better present and future as directly as possible

It's tempting to suggest our energies could be better used somewhere other than helping betrayers heal. After all, shouldn't they suffer for their wrongdoing? It's a valid consideration and one that bears exploration. Several dynamics come into play when considering this issue. Let's start with numbers.

I tend to be more artsy than mathematical so I won't burden you with charts and tables. These are a few figures that I find staggering when I consider the potential cost of unhealed betrayers.

At the time of this writing:

- 2% of the adult male population of the US is incarcerated
- There are 7 million children in the US with one or more parent in prison; without intervention 70% of those children will end up behind bars themselves
- Infidelity occurs in 60%-80% of marriages in the US

- Sexual addiction is estimated to affect up to 8% of adult males—that's 15 million men worldwide
- Drunk drivers killed 16,885 people in the US in 2005
- 80% - 98% of children worldwide experience physical punishment in their homes, with a third of those experiencing severe punishment with the use of implements

Turning a blind eye toward the need for betrayers to heal leaves a gaping hole in our society. Human beings are tribal by nature. We are programmed by our biology to seek deep connection with those around us. It makes sense in the evolutionary picture; in our earliest days our greatest enemies were large cats with sharp teeth that could run faster and see in the dark. Alone we didn't stand a chance. Banded together we survived as a species. Our biochemical make-up made sure we banded together by giving us an internal reward system: pleasure. We feel good—at peace, contented, fulfilled—when we are connected to others. We feel isolated, lonely, sad, and uncomfortable in our own skin when we are disconnected from those around us.

Betrayal is the great disconnector. The human system is an amazing thing. Not only do we feel good when we're connected to those around us and bad when we're not, our brains are wired so that we experience regret, remorse, shame, and ultimately self-loathing when we cause harm to others—to our tribe. Regret and remorse are the gifts of our emotional system poking and prodding us to make things right, to reconnect by mending fences. Shame and self-loathing are what happen when we ignore those messages, cutting ourselves off even further.

Those are, of course, major, life-altering betrayal events. As staggering as those numbers are in highlighting the issue of betrayal, they don't necessarily relate directly to the kinds of betrayal we might be responsible for in our daily lives. There aren't Justice Bureau, MADD, or other official stats for the smaller betrayals. No one counts and quantifies gossip, family feuds, workplace sabotage, or harsh words between loved ones. There's no tracking system to tell us how many times we're rude to wait-staff, brusque with our children, or sloppy in our work obligations.

And yet, life is in the small things. Most of us will never attend a 12-Step group and even fewer of us will be faced with the prospect of Restorative Justice. We can be deeply grateful for that. Every one of us will, simply by virtue of being human, find ourselves betraying our inner values in one way or another. Virtually every adult has moments they are not proud to recall. Most of those times are mundane events where the moment got away from us and we acted without thinking. Some of those times are more painful memories of betrayal—those skeletons in the closet of our memories that we try desperately to avoid and that seem to rattle loudest in the wee hours just before dawn. Betrayal healing is for everyone.

Ignoring the need to mend fences—to reconnect—creates deeper levels of disconnect. The more disconnected we become, the less likely we are to interact with openness and authenticity. We create a downward spiral that ripples outward.

Amber called her children on Christmas Day. She had not seen them in close to a year and the last time they'd spoken was sometime in the late summer. She dreaded making the call. The children were full of happy chatter about their gifts, their friends, and their social life. Amber couldn't think of a thing to say and quickly made an excuse to hang up. All the while, her stomach churned and an inner dialogue ran through her head telling her what a bad parent she was. She was embarrassed to share in her children's holiday happiness.

His Holiness the Dalai Lama tells us, "Our every act has a universal dimension." Amber's inability to move beyond her guilt and toward reconnection illustrates the validity of the statement. The negative diatribe in her head was so loud she couldn't hear the happy voices of her children. All she heard was condemnation, her own unworthiness. Her girls hung up the phone feeling uneasy and discontent with the outcome of the conversation—the day seemed flatter and duller. The effect rippled out to their father and friends and in smaller ripples to the people around them. Amber's unhealed betrayal moved in subtle waves and touched everyone. Our own unhealed betrayals do the same—as do all unhealed betrayals.

Joanna Bare, physicist, poet, and coach, tells us that when viewed through the lens of physics, the separateness we take as fact is in reality nothing more than illusion. "I and Thou…. We are One" she writes. How profound that is on so many levels. When we harm another we harm ourselves. When others are harmed, so too, are we. Disconnect separates us from the greater Oneness. Healing must lie in reestablishing connection—recreating Oneness. Atonement, making amends, can be written and experienced as At-One-Ment. Betrayal healing removes our self-imposed barriers to connection and oneness and brings us back to wholeness. We might even say, to holiness.

Our profound desire for connection is what motivates us to ethical behavior. We all want to feel connected in a deep way. We are at our very best when we view the world as "We" instead of "We and They." Tolerance and peace exist only in a state of connectedness. This is true whether we are discussing family dynamics or global interactions.

Lisa started making her annual list of invitees for the big holiday gathering. Active in church and volunteer work, the list was extensive. She hummed a little as she clattered the keys on her computer. Making a list, checking it twice: close friends, grown children, church friends, friends from this or that volunteer group, family… her fingers stopped moving. Family. She took a deep breath and added her ex-husband to the list. In more than ten years he had never so much as set foot in her home; one more baby step toward healing.

After days of cleaning and cooking, the date finally arrived. Scrumptious smells filled the house. People arrived bearing gifts of food and drink. Happy chatter and laughter filled every corner. And there in the mingling groups of gathered friends was Lisa's ex standing next to his tall daughter, catching up with his former in-laws. The old hurts were not completely forgotten, but a great many fences were mended that day. Tensions were eased. Some of the holes in Lisa's children's lives were filled.

Betrayal healing creates interesting dynamics. As Lisa's former husband took a risk and allowed her to share her inner wounds, he also let go of some of his own. We would, almost universally, see him as the betrayed party and rightfully so. Yet, when her ex-husband reacted with anger, harsh words, and mild vengeance during their divorce, he perpetrated some betrayals of his own. Lisa's openness and vulnerability created space for him to look more closely at his past behavior and to heal. Their joint willingness to recreate connection flowed to their children. It will continue to ripple subtly through the lives of everyone they touch. Which is, of course, everyone.

Adam is not someone most of us want to know. He said, once, "No one wants to hear that murder hurts the murderer, too." He's right about that. Our inner horror of betrayal makes us want to turn our faces from the worst betrayal—violent personal crime. We don't want to know about his pain—we instinctively pull away from someone who violates our tribal drive for connection and survival in the worst possible way, by taking an innocent life. We are tempted to suggest Adam doesn't deserve to heal. Perhaps he doesn't. But we deserve his healing.

Most criminals, including Adam, will one day be released from prison. Our safety and that of our loved ones depends on Adam's—and others like him—ability to fully face his acts of betrayal, heal the profound disconnect, and move to a place of wholeness. If our every act has a universal dimension, then when we create space for Adam to heal we participate in creating a safer world. When we see the Adams of the world as human, we create space for our own healing.

Facing our wrongdoings, experiencing empathy for those we've harmed, sharing our humanness and being validated, and then making amends, is sometimes met with glitches. A little introspection and creativity goes a long way.

Amber hated being stuck. Beneath her present state of what looked like an emotional jellyfish, Amber had been born with a sturdy backbone. Awakening suddenly one morning, she burst fully into the realization that she alone was responsible for her healing. Instead of relying on others to validate her, she realized she could do it for herself. Grabbing her fuzzy old robe, she went to the mirror that stood in the corner and, feeling a bit like some folk tale figure, taking a deep breath and spoke aloud.

"I was hurt and angry and I wanted to hurt him in return," she said. She could feel the tears stinging the place behind her nose. "I fell in love, and I'm not sorry I did. I am sorry for the way it happened. I ran away and I hurt a lot of people. I hurt my babies," the tears flowed now, as they had never been allowed to before. "I hurt my new marriage because of my guilt and triggering. And I hurt someone I once loved very deeply."

Taking a deep breath, she paused. Then she looked squarely into her own face; this was the hardest part. "Yes, you did," she said. "And you betrayed your own beliefs and values about family and love and honor." She choked a little, but she was determined to finish. "They didn't deserve what you did. You didn't deserve what you did. It's been a wedge between all of you for years." A long pause.

"I can work on the wedge, I think... I will."

Over coffee that morning Amber wrote a letter to her children. To the point and free of any hint of self-pity, she expressed a desire to be more active in their lives. She knew from experience that apologizing embarrassed them, so instead she spoke of her own embarrassment and feelings of uneasiness and asked for their help in creating a closer relationship. Within a year Amber made a trip back to her hometown for an extended visit. It was hard work—some of it painful, much of it bittersweet—and every bit of it was worthwhile. Amber still feels stuck sometimes, and she vows to continue to "work on the wedge" a little bit at a time. Like Adam, she's doing the best she can with what she has. It's not perfect—and that's all right.

Healing relationships is all about recreating the layers of connection. Trust, safety, fulfillment, and contentment—all emanate from profound connection. To look at relationship healing only from the position of the betrayed is to ignore an enormous piece of the bigger picture. Relationships are spiraling dynamics created with every interaction. Profound connection requires the engagement of whole persons. Betrayed and betrayer participate by first healing their own wounds and then by healing the relationship. The betrayed can trust again only when the betrayer is trustworthy. The betrayer can only be trustworthy when actively connected to the greater whole.

Relationship healing efforts that focus solely on the needs of the betrayed may require or anticipate participation from the betrayer in order to make the betrayed feel safer or more connected. Connection, though, is a two-way street. It's impossible to be intimately connected to someone who is not available. Authentic healing within relationships must be holistic. If the betrayer remains locked behind walls of shame and guilt, any actions taken to appease the betrayed will be superficial at best. Conversely, if the betrayer steps out of the self-absorbed place of shame and guilt and into empathy for the betrayed, the behavior will naturally be in accord. Actions taken from this place are healing and connecting at a deep level. Not only will the betrayed feel safer and more connected—they will be so. Betrayal healing for the betrayer is the essential first step in healing relationships. Healing relationships is the essential first step for healing the world.

About
Penny R Tupy

Penny R Tupy didn't write this bio; it's not the usual bio in any case. Sure, I'll tell you important things, like how she's been a marriage coach for this whole millennium, specializing in topics that make most folks very uncomfortable. Before that, she had a great career in printing. But that's dull and you probably don't really care. I'm going to tell you what you really need to know about. I'm going to tell you about Penny the person, not Penny the persona.

Penny cares. She cares more deeply than she lets on most of the time, and yet that's the first thing that'll hit you when you talk to her. She really cares about what matters, and doesn't care at all about what doesn't: the color of your skin, the gender of your partner, the flavor of your religion. Those are interesting to talk about on an intellectual level. But they don't really matter. Your integrity matters. The people you love? They matter.

She blends her love of people with a sharp intellect. She'll dissect your cherished beliefs and thought patterns, pull out the important bits, and from them build a new structure that you're sure you didn't think of yourself. And yet, the solution is perfectly **you**. Better yet, the solution is ethical. She studies ethics the way some of us read the funny pages when we were ten.

She knows the scripts of marital agony. She's been there. She knows why a betrayed spouse cannot get away from that awful question, "Why won't she just come home and forget about him?" She knows why an affair partner can say, honestly, "I never meant to hurt her." She knows, too, how someone who's having an affair can plan to leave his wife and redecorate the house with her at the same time. She understands the twisted mirror affect of addiction, the distorted reality of abuse. She has an uncanny ability to synthesize broad categories of information and, from that, come up with something completely new. You'll walk away asking, "Wow. How come no one else ever told me that?"

In a single hour on the phone—or in a friendship—with Penny, you may cover modern mythological archetypes, the biochemistry of love, recent work on healing, ethical constructs from Eastern and Western traditions, and how to use a condom. Best of all, at the end of it, you'll know why those concepts are important in your life and for your unique situation—and you'll have started to learn how to hold onto yourself as you grow into behaving with empowerment in your relationships.

Penny is an ordained minister in a religion that faces tremendous discrimination and prejudice. She drives two hours each way to a high security prison every Wednesday night (it's a good night to reach her on her cell phone) to minister to the "lost boys" (as she affectionately calls them) who let her care for some part of their souls. She spends many hours in both the adult and juvenile corrections system, giving her time to people whom many consider lost causes. She enjoys every minute of it.

In her spare time, Penny founded and runs Save Your Marriage Central, Incorporated, the SYMC Global Village (a non-profit corporation dedicated to the community support needed to save a marriage), and started the Marriage Fidelity Day campaign, a day to celebrate and act on commitment to marital vows. She'll speak to you with passion and conviction on the topic of marriage, ethics, and why your vows matter. And she'll awaken in you a belief in your own vows that you never knew you had. At the end of the day, you'll know why you meant it when you said yes.

Penny has been published in local media, interviewed across the country regarding Marriage Fidelity Day, and appeared on the NBC Today Show as a relationship expert.

To contact Penny call 651-775-8302 or email her at penny.tupy@ symcinc.com.

Fifty Ways to Leave Your Lover: How Divorce Coaching Helps Relationships

By Kathleen Oqueli McGraw

"CHILDREN BEGIN BY LOVING THEIR PARENTS; AS THEY GROW OLDER THEY JUDGE THEM; SOMETIMES THEY FORGIVE THEM." ~ OSCAR WILDE

Leigh saw the return address from her classmate and eagerly opened the letter. Ten years had passed since she and her four friends from high school had made a pact to stay in touch. So much had changed in that time. Memories came flooding back to her as she recalled each of those friends.

The captain of the cheerleading squad, Leigh was the peacemaker and was known as "The Glue" that kept everyone together. Royce, her boyfriend throughout high school, was the quarterback of the football team. Although they called him "The Partier," he graduated at the top of their class. When he chose a different college than she, the distance was too much for their relationship, and their lives moved on. She smiled as she remembered their times together. She had thought of him often in the intervening years.

Her best friend, Jackie, was the dreamer in the group, "The Drama Queen" literally and by nickname. She was the lead in every theatrical production and had aspirations of being a famous movie star, refusing to allow anything to get in her way, including love.

As Leigh reminisced about her time with Jackie, Stanley popped into her mind. Stanley, "The Bookworm," had a secret crush on Jackie, and she felt the same about him. But for some reason, although everyone knew they liked each other, no one ever talked about it. Stanley spent so much time studying and in math league competitions, it seemed he cared more for his books than a relationship with Jackie.

As Leigh thought about the relationships in her group, her memories finally led to Gustavo, the captain of their soccer team, the playboy they called, "The Latin Lover." Gustavo had numerous girlfriends and was never without a female at his side. He was determined to be known as soccer's "Most Eligible Bachelor," and left a trail of broken hearts everywhere he went.

Leigh's thoughts moved forward to her current life in Fontainebleau, a neighborhood in New Orleans. She met her husband when both were college freshmen, fell in love, and married soon after graduating. Leigh's ambition was to become a marriage and family therapist, while her husband pursued his dream of becoming the president of a company. After completing her doctorate, she was hired as a relationship therapist on a local radio talk show, and soon gained a position at the local university. No matter how successful her life was she always wanted more.

Meanwhile, her husband worked his way up the ladder at a large company, and although he had not reached his goal of becoming company president, he was very successful. Working six days a week, going to work early and leaving late, Leigh began to suspect that her husband was having an affair with his secretary.

Concerned that she would lose her credibility as an expert in marriages and relationships, Leigh was afraid to confront him. She wasn't sure she could take her own advice to callers on her radio show: "No matter what, for the sake of the children, try and work it out."

Like many of her own clients, Leigh began to blame herself for his indiscretions, that he cheated because she was never there for him, too busy focusing on her own profession. She decided not to leave him, as she could not do that to the children.

To show her support and lead him back to her, she celebrated his many successes, extolling his virtues at every company social event, cocktail, and holiday party. Her husband was soon promoted to president and his secretary became his executive assistant.

Leigh swallowed her pride and although she was not happy, she endured. She felt there was too much to lose to do anything else.

***

Royce opened his reunion invitation on the deck of his spacious home in Lakeview. He couldn't believe 10 years had passed since he left high school. Like Leigh, the letter brought a flood of memories, mostly of the years since he finished college at the top of his class.

Royce was hired by a leading advertising firm, rising quickly in the company. He thought back to the first company holiday party where he met the date of a colleague—a direct competitor for every account he acquired. The colleague's date worked for his company's competition. Within a year, Royce left the company to start his own advertising firm. He took most of his clients and his colleague's girlfriend with him.

With his company doing well, he married his newly won girlfriend, and three wonderful children soon filled their beautiful home. Because of his success, they decided his wife would stay home and raise their children. She loved her life as a stay-at-home mother, and her life revolved around her kids.

With his company growing by leaps and bounds, Royce opened a second office, requiring more travel and time away from home, draining his energy and keeping him from taking time for himself. Hoping for more support from home, he hired a nanny and housekeeper to free up time for his wife to work with him. However, instead of asking her directly to consider working with him, he felt that if she worked less at home, she would get the hint. That never happened.

Instead, she demanded more of his time in helping her with the children. He couldn't find the time, and eventually they grew apart. Not communicating their wants and needs, they ended up resenting each other.

Although their home was immaculate and their children had the best of everything, they were like ships passing in the night. Their picture perfect life was a lie.

***

The invitation for his class reunion was a welcome relief to Stanley. The day before, he was confronted with news of an entirely different sort. What had gone wrong in his marriage to cause such betrayal? He searched his memory for a reason for his wife's actions.

After college, Stanley spent hours in the local library, researching information for his first book. He knew where everything in the library was, including the librarian. They started spending time outside the library together, and eventually married in front of the Library of Congress. A son followed, a brilliant child named Dewey.

He soon became a published author and they were able to buy a lovely home in Gentilly. Stanley started a new book, returning often to the library for research. His wife argued that if he focused on promoting his first book, he could take a break from writing. The truth was she wanted to be the center of his attention, fearing his second book was her biggest competition. She complained that they had not made enough money off the initial book. He just wanted to write another one.

This went on for months, with his wife focusing more and more on money and their lack of it. Stanley took care of paying the bills in the house and kept them on a budget. His first book was doing well and he was about to receive an advance for his second, a history of the Federal Emergency Management Agency, a definite best seller in the post-Katrina era. He couldn't understand her obsession and nagging.

Then yesterday, while balancing their checkbook and reviewing their financial statements, he called the bank to straighten out some apparent errors. The gentleman on the phone said something about having obtained a "line of credit" and a "second mortgage on the house."

At that moment, his wife walked into the house, asking, "Honey, do you notice anything different about the way I look?"

It suddenly all made sense, the new clothes, the new shoes, the new car, the new look. His wife had gone behind his back, secured large loans, and had a complete makeover. She concealed it all from him, hiding the growing stack of bills.

In his dismay and hurt, the reunion invitation was a welcome distraction.

***

The arrival of the invitation was much different for Gustavo. He was elated for more than one reason. He would have great news to share with his old friends. Had it really been so long since they were together? So much had transpired in those ten years.

After leaving high school, Gustavo earned a soccer scholarship. He soon became a professional, earning wealth and fame. He looked good, played well, and had countless fans, thanks to the media.

Invited to an interview for a prominent sports magazine, he accepted the request. Although he was prepared to answer any question asked, he found himself speechless when the most beautiful woman he had ever seen walked in. Cool and professional, the journalist seemed unflustered by his good looks, charms, and accomplishments. Intrigued by her aloofness, he felt compelled to ask her for a date. Surprisingly, she accepted.

After a hot and steamy first date, they were soon spending every day together. She wrote numerous exclusives on Gustavo for the magazine, and he devoted all of his time to her. After a whirlwind romance, with her traveling with the soccer team, he proudly introduced her to his parents. They were elated, seeing the possibility of grandchildren in the near future.

They were married in an elaborate and expensive wedding. After buying a large and exquisite home in English Turn, his next concern was filling it with children. She, on the other hand, was happy with what they had. His wife continued her work, but no longer traveled with him or attended his games.

His wife became the lead sports journalist at the magazine and traveled the country interviewing other sports figures, loving the attention. Gustavo suspected there was more going on than interviews, and demanded she turn down new assignments. He gave her an ultimatum, "Shape up or ship out."

She promised to be a better spouse and work on their marriage. She traveled less, stayed home more, and accepted fewer assignments. Their relationship seemed to improve. She was home more, but was focused on a new rising star, a linebacker with the New Orleans Saints football team. He became her feature story in most of her articles.

The day before the invitation arrived, his wife was feeling ill. When the doctor told them she was pregnant, Gustavo began crying tears of joy. His wife was crying, too, but hers were tears of sorrow. Gustavo was too happy to notice the difference. And, she was too afraid of telling him the truth—the baby may not be his, and their marriage was over.

***

Jackie stared at the invitation in her hand. Just the day before, she received both the best and worst news of her life. Now, she had a chance to see her old friends, and a mixture of relief and confusion filled her mind.

Why hadn't she seen the signs? She searched her memories for pieces to the puzzle.

Shortly after high school, Jackie auditioned for every movie, commercial, play, and street performance in town. After finding a temporary job as a waitress to pay the bills, she realized that to accomplish her dreams, she would need an agent. She met with many possible agents, and finally met "The One." He was handsome, charming, and could spot talent from miles away.

Her agent worked hard for her, sending her to many auditions. She soon realized she was falling in love with him, but never felt the feeling was mutual. Despite the lack of personal attention from him, when she wasn't with him, she constantly thought of him.

With his efforts, Jackie began to get call backs for acting parts and quit her day job. She soon became his sole client, taking it as a sign of his love and devotion. Sensing it was time to make her feelings known, she told him how she felt about him. With no shock or surprise, he asked her to marry him.

Within days, they returned from their honeymoon, a disappointment for Jackie. They had not made love. They would hug and kiss, but go no further. With their romantic getaway, she was on cloud nine, believing everything in her life was falling into place. They moved into a stylish home in the Vieux Carré, fit for a movie star. Nevertheless, something was just not right.

Jackie assumed her husband was inexperienced and thus she would have to take the initiative. Slowly, but soon. Perhaps, she thought, he suffered from performance anxiety.

One day, her husband brought home a fire fighter costume. He asked her to put it on and said it was for the next role she was going to play. When she returned with the costume on, he was very excited. That night they made love for the first time.

Every night, when he asked her to dress in different costumes, she would agree to role play any scene. She was an actress, and if that was what it took to please her husband, she could do it. She started to bring home her own, more feminine costumes, but he wasn't interested in anything but first responder uniforms and construction worker costumes.

Then yesterday, as they sat down to dinner, they both had news for each other. Jackie exclaimed, "We're going to have a baby!" Her husband froze, stunned and speechless. He finally whispered through a dry throat, "I'm gay."

Jackie screamed, knowing it was true. She was no longer in denial and neither was he.

***

Leigh was the first to arrive at the reunion, standing outside the banquet hall waiting for the others to arrive. She left her husband at home, wanting to reconnect to her past and temporarily let go of the present. She wasn't the only one to come unescorted. Stanley, Gustavo, and Royce soon arrived, each one solo. Jackie was the last to appear, making a grand entrance, lavish and alone.

They were delighted to see each other, and quickly began to reconnect and renew old bonds. "Laissez les bons temps rouler! (Let the good times roll!)" yelled Royce, and they all made their way into the reunion.

They partied all night, without a care in the world, or so it seemed. They shared their successes, talked about their families and professions, and recalled shared memories. After the reunion, they checked into the Hotel Monteleone, then staggered down Bourbon Street. Jackie kept a motherly eye on the gang as she pretended to drink along with the group.

The morning after, each one began to share their personal stories, revealing their problems, disappointments, and less than perfect marriages. Long suppressed feelings and rekindled emotions were renewed.

They talked about their futures and devised plans. They were each going to end their marriages in their own way as soon as they returned home. Like they did so long ago, they agreed to support each other as they started anew.

"Just Drop Off The Key, Lee"

Leigh walked into her husband's office, dropped off the key to the beach house, and marched out. She called a moving company, had them pack her husband's items, and sent him on his way. She was no longer going to fool herself by "working" on their marriage. However, she was not going to give her husband a divorce either. She decided they would be legally separated, live in separate homes, and publicly act as though everything was fine. Their professions would remain intact, but their family would not.

They remained legally separated for years, resulting in no real sense of closure for them or the children. This was a serious disservice to their children who continued to believe their parents were going to reconcile. The parents avoided going back to court, maintaining the façade, but their children ended up confused and in therapy.

"You Don't Need To Be Coy, Roy"

Royce returned home and informed his wife he was filing for a divorce. His wife felt wounded and angry. She threatened him with never seeing his children again and having to pay huge amounts of child support and alimony. He knew he had a fight on his hands and was determined to win. He found the best adversarial attorney in town, determined to intimidate his wife. He vowed she would receive nothing.

Their divorce was filled with conflict. They argued with and demeaned each other in front of the children. Their attorneys acted like "hired guns" fighting to defeat the "opponent." The children were pulled back and forth between the parents. They each spent a fortune on attorney and court costs. In the end their children suffered, acting out in school, being suspended numerous times, and sneaking out of their homes in the middle of the night.

"Just Slip Out The Back, Jack"

Jackie went home in the middle of the night and packed her bags. She knew she could not have a public divorce, feeling it would humiliate her for others to find out her husband was gay. Jackie decided she would not let her husband destroy her career. She wrote him a note explaining her need for a divorce, and asked for custody of their child. Jackie's husband felt as though he had to agree to her terms, because he was not ready for his sexual orientation to be revealed to the public either.

They met for coffee one night, negotiated, and hashed out many of the details. They went to court to present their "kitchen table divorce" agreements to the judge. Jackie and her husband both represented themselves in the divorce and neither of them hired an attorney. For years after the divorce, both parents held grudges and wondered if they had made the best deal. Their child resented his parents' inability to face reality and to stop living in denial. The child grew up repeating many of his parents' mistakes, resulting in difficulty with romantic relationships.

"Make A New Plan, Stan"

Stanley and his wife went to a family mediator to facilitate the discussion of their parenting plan and their division of property. The mediator brought both parents closer toward agreement through this form of alternative dispute resolution. The mediator was a neutral third party and could not give advice or advocate for either parties' side. They came to agree on some of the issues, but not all. The problem was that both were advocating for themselves and not for the "best interests of the child." They went to court, where the judge decided the remaining issues regarding their child and the division of property.

They had difficulty sticking to their mediated agreement. There was no follow up with their mediator after their case had been "resolved." Their relationship continued to be high conflict, with their child caught in the middle. He grew up lacking confidence and self esteem.

"Hop On The Bus, Gus"

Gustavo and his wife went to attorneys who specialized in Collaborative Divorce™. The attorneys explained to the couple that the process is a multi-disciplinary team approach to separation and divorce. It includes attorneys, divorce coaches, a financial specialist, and a child specialist working together as co-equals. They worked with the team and did not have to step foot in a courtroom. They learned that a Collaborative Divorce™ is a transparent process and both of them would have to cooperate in order for it to work. Gustavo's wife understood her dishonesty could no longer continue.

They realized, with the help of their divorce coaches, that even though they were no longer together romantically, they would continue to have a co-parenting relationship for the rest of their child's life. Their divorce coaches worked with the couple to improve their communication and negotiation skills. The coaches helped them to co-parent in ways that were better for the child. They learned how to work together and have a civil relationship for the sake of the child. Divorce coaches supported the parents, guiding them to stay on track, helping them work together, and providing resources to improve their co-parenting skills. Their child grew up to learn and demonstrate effective communication and conflict resolution skills in all of his relationships, both professional and personal.

Epilogue

Separation and divorce are prevalent in our society. According to the National Center for Health Statistics, the percentage of first marriages that end in divorce is 50 percent, with that figure increasing with each remarriage. Separation and divorce are life-altering experiences and can be traumatic, especially if there are children in the family. According to the National Center for Health Statistics, the number of children in new divorces each year is over 1 million.

Traditionally, relationship coaches have assisted clients who were working on their love life to remain a couple, most often focusing on strengthening relationships. Clients often include those who are single, dating, or married. Clients also include individuals focusing on relationships between parents and children, friends, and in business. However, another aspect of relationship coaching is working with separating or divorcing couples, as well as couples coping with an affair. This type of relationship coach is more often referred to as a divorce coach.

There are many skills that add to a divorce coach's effectiveness, including background, education, and experience in:
- professional coaching
- communication styles and skills
- family systems theory
- individual and family life cycles and development
- assessment of individual and family strengths
- assessment and challenges of family dynamics during separation and divorce
- knowledge of the challenges of restructuring families after separation and divorce.

Collaborative Divorce™ organizations also request that divorce coaches be licensed mental health professionals, have training in mediation, a basic understanding of family law in his or her own jurisdiction, and interdisciplinary collaborative divorce training.

As the song says, "There are fifty ways to leave your lover." This chapter looks at five methods used to end marriages:

- permanent legal separation
- litigation with attorneys
- litigation without the assistance of attorneys
- mediation
- Collaborative Divorce™ with the assistance of trained professionals, such as divorce coaches

Collaborative divorces are viewed as the preferred choice, as it is the least adversarial of the five methods. However, divorce coaches can be used to improve the outcomes of couples who mediate, litigate, or separate.

Divorce signifies the end of a romantic relationship and is many times the beginning of a co-parenting relationship between two separate households. With the assistance of a divorce coach, co-parents can have a civil relationship and learn effective self-management, conflict resolution, communication, and co-parenting skills. In addition, parents learn not to use their children as weapons in the negotiation process, and to do what is in their children's best interest.

Why is a chapter on divorce included in a book about vibrant and lasting relationships? Because, there are many instances of divorce when there are children involved, making the parental relationship a lasting one, both with the children and with the co-parent.

Relationship skills are essential, and the more support and knowledge each participant has, the more each generation will benefit. A divorce/relationship coach can help provide that support and knowledge as families work through this difficult transition.

---

* Words taken from Paul Simon's song "Fifty Ways to Leave Your Lover" 1975 from album *Still Crazy After All These Years* on the Warner Bros. label.

About
Kathleen Oqueli McGraw

Kathleen Oqueli McGraw is the founding partner of Kathleen McGraw, LCSW & Associates, LLC. She is also the executive director of the Mariposa Institute for Families, Parenting, and Children™. She specializes in providing mental health, mediation, facilitation, and coaching services for children and adults living in high conflict families.

Kathleen received her Master of Social Work from Tulane University. She has a Master of Public Health in *Community Health Sciences* and *Maternal and Child Health* from Tulane University's School of Public Health and Tropical Medicine. She is currently completing her doctoral dissertation for her Ph.D. in Social Work from Tulane University.

A licensed clinical social worker and a psychotherapist, she provides therapy to children, adolescents, and adults, and works with individuals, couples, groups, and families. She is a referral member of the Louisiana Association of Clinical Social Workers and the National Association of Social Workers.

Kathleen is a family mediator, trained by Loyola Law School, and a juvenile mediator, trained by the Child Advocacy Mediation Program of the Louisiana Supreme Court. She mediates in family, juvenile, and "Child in Need of Care" cases. She is a board member of the Family Mediation Council of Louisiana and the Juvenile Mediation Council of Louisiana. She is honored to be listed in the Louisiana State Bar Association's Journal titled, "Who's Who in ADR 2007."

Trained at CoachU, Kathleen is a life, relationship, communication, and parenting coach, also providing coaching to children, teens, and college students. She belongs to the International Coach Federation and the International Association of Coaches.

Kathleen is a Collaborative Divorce™ Coach and Child Specialist, as she advocates for alternative dispute resolution services that assist families in resolving conflict. She is a member of the Collaborative Professional Group of Southeast Louisiana and the International Academy of Collaborative Professionals.

Trained by the Association of Family and Conciliation Courts through Loyola Law School, Kathleen provides child custody evaluations and is a parenting coordinator. She was appointed to the Louisiana State Law Institute's Committee on Parenting Coordination, and developed the statutes that define the roles and qualifications of parenting coordinators in Louisiana.

Kathleen is also a professional trainer, speaker, writer, and group facilitator. She co–authored the book, *101 Great Ways to Improve Your Life, Volume II*. She has given presentations and facilitated workshops at both national and international conferences.

Since Hurricanes Katrina and Rita, Kathleen has facilitated workshops focused on the trauma recovery process for adults, children, and communities after a disaster. She has worked extensively with families, school teachers and counselors, first responders, and community organizers in the areas of conflict and dispute resolution, anger management, relationships, and communication skills needed after life traumas. Kathleen has also facilitated several city-wide meetings in New Orleans organized by AmericaSpeaks and the United New Orleans Plan (UNOP) to aid in the recovery and rebuilding of New Orleans and the surrounding communities.

Kathleen was awarded the "Great Women of the 21st Century Eclipse Award," which is given to only 1000 women worldwide.

Kathleen McGraw, LCSW & Associates, LLC has two locations to serve you:

3350 Ridgelake Drive, Suite 245, Metairie, LA 70002 USA
(504) 836-3883
and
943 Paul Maillard Road, Luling, LA 70070 USA
(985) 785-9300
Email kathleen@McGrawandAssociates or
visit www.McGrawandAssociates.com

Connecting with Co-Workers

By Deb Yeagle

"DEPENDENT PEOPLE NEED OTHERS TO GET WHAT THEY WANT. INDEPENDENT PEOPLE CAN GET WHAT THEY WANT THROUGH THEIR OWN EFFORTS. INTERDEPENDENT PEOPLE COMBINE THEIR OWN EFFORTS WITH THE EFFORTS OF OTHERS TO ACHIEVE THEIR GREATEST SUCCESS." ~ STEPHEN COVEY

What does it take to build networks, alliances, and bonds with peers and co-workers? Six ambitious and committed employees, with similar backgrounds, education, and experience, use different communication styles and interpersonal skills that many times hinder development of vibrant and lasting relationships with co-workers. Although they are alike in many ways, Elliott, Frank, Gina, Haley, Irene, and Jake each interact with co-workers in very different ways. Let's look at how these employees overcame numerous obstacles to build trust, collaboration, and cooperation, in place of competition, to strengthen their relationships, and ultimately their organization.

Elliott is referred to by his co-workers as a "lone wolf." He works independently because he does not trust his peers. This lack of trust originated early in his career when one of his co-workers took credit for an idea Elliott shared with him. Since then, he decided that he would avoid the cutthroat work environment by taking on the most difficult assignments himself and working hard to complete them on his own. Elliott feels by working independently, he will avoid being victimized by another co-worker and be way ahead of the competition for career advancement.

Frank interacts very little with his peers. Instead, he invests his time with several senior employees that he has carefully selected as role models. He has several mentors who provide him career advice, help him handle various situations at work, and teach him the "unwritten" rules of success in the organization. Although he works well with his peers when he needs to complete team projects, he devotes most of his time to developing deeper relationships with his senior mentors. Frank feels that the key to advancing his career is learning the ropes from the more experienced, senior employees of the organization.

Gina is extremely dedicated and loyal to her boss. She does not consider herself a brown-noser, but she works hard to manage her boss as an escape from the competitive, backbiting atmosphere in her office. She communicates daily with her boss, keeping her informed and offering to help out as needed. Gina feels that continuing to nurture the excellent relationship she has with her superior will enable her to climb the career ladder quicker than her peers.

Haley works well on a team and has close personal relationships with everyone in her work group. Haley's team is so close-knit, in fact, that it is viewed as a clique by other work groups in the organization. Haley supports the co-workers on her team, and defends and protects them from other work groups. At times, she instigates rivalries with other work groups because she feels that competition is healthy for the organization. She is so confident in her team's abilities that she knows the competition will ultimately put her team in the limelight and help advance the individual members' careers.

Irene is everyone's friend at work. She avoids getting involved in office politics by trying to get along well with everybody. Since she is quick to please and appease, she finds herself making secret agreements and alliances with work groups that are at odds. Irene feels that if she can remain neutral and avoid conflict by being everyone's friend, then she can breeze along her career path without being scarred by backbiting co-workers and without being labeled as belonging to any particular camp in the office.

Jake spends a lot of time outside of his team talking with employees in other work groups. He keeps his team members informed of what he learns from these interactions about other parts of the organization. During team meetings, Jake is usually the one who helps resolve conflict by facilitating and negotiating. Sometimes Jake invites employees from other work groups to team meetings if he thinks they might have a stake in what his team is doing. He inspires and motivates his team members to drive them toward meeting their goals. Jake believes that to be successful, he must lead his peers to be successful, helping them develop and nurture their working relationships while continuing to build and maintain his network of co-workers.

Of these six employees, which one is building the most vital relationships at work that will lead to the most successful career? Which one "gets it"?

Because he connects with his co-workers and peers, values their contributions, and inspires cooperation among them to achieve success together, Jake is well on his way to having the most successful career. While Elliott's work ethic is commendable, he must still learn to work as part of a team. Frank's relationships with senior mentors are undoubtedly fruitful, but without establishing deeper relationships with his peers, Frank has limited opportunities to build on his successes. Gina's ability to manage up is a valuable skill, but she must balance the time spent nurturing the relationship with her boss and time needed to develop relationships with her co-workers and peers.

Unlike, Elliott, Frank, and Gina, Haley understands the value of building relationships with her peers. However, Haley's antagonistic demeanor with other work groups is counter-productive since it does not promote cooperation and collaboration within the organization. Like Haley, Irene has built strong bonds with her peers, but her tendency to avoid conflict with co-workers and her inability to take a stand limits her career advancement.

Relationships with peers are more important than any other relationship in the work environment. Since peers are viewed as the main source of competition in regard to career advancement, it is human nature to avoid developing relationships with them. This competitive, backbiting atmosphere at work breeds a lack of trust among co-workers. What does it take by someone like Jake to overcome these tendencies to develop these relationships?

First, it takes being comfortable with yourself and having the knowledge, skills, and willingness to connect to others. Managing relationships with others requires you to have the ability to manage yourself. The ability to relate to others requires empathy—simply caring, treating people with respect, and letting others know they are important to you is the foundation for building relationships based on mutual trust. **Relationships with your peers and co-workers based on trust pave the way toward cooperation and collaboration instead of competition.**

Jake's ability to develop relationships by demonstrating empathy and trustworthiness allows him to build networks, alliances, and bonds with peers and co-workers.

Jake's first step to ensuring career success is through his ability to develop connections with co-workers and peers, but he realizes that developing deeper, more meaningful relationships requires an additional skill—the ability to acknowledge, accept, and appreciate the differences in others.

Beyond the relationship with self and learning how to build trust, it takes being skilled both in valuing diversity and in influencing others to achieve shared success.

The Value of Diversity

Finding common ground is the way that most connections with co-workers are developed. Sharing like experiences and interests helps build rapport. It is also important to discover differences, and then learn to respect those differences and apply them to the greater good of the team or organization.

Jake has a natural ability to get along with many different kinds of people. But what if you aren't blessed with that type of personality? It is still possible to learn how to build bonds with anyone, whether or not you have discovered common ground.

Here's how:

1. **Keep your eyes and ears open.** Be aware of other people. Watch and observe. Listen. You will learn so much more about other people by simply tuning into what they're

doing and saying. Use this as an entrée into conversations and seize opportunities to connect.

2. **Learn to give and take.** Without being overbearing or trying to force the connection, give a little of yourself to others —open up, show your vulnerability, and make yourself available. You don't have to bare your soul, but you can't build connections without making yourself accessible. When others do the same for you, show your *acceptance* and *appreciation*. It takes two to connect.

3. **Let go of the past.** If you have a history of bad blood with someone that may prevent future connections, then wipe the slate clean. You can't move forward if you're always looking back. Hanging on to the past will limit you in so many ways; not only are you missing out on potential relationships, but your bitterness is bound to eventually rule and ruin your life. Forgive and forget.

4. **Keep an open mind.** Everyone is entitled to their opinion. Value others' opinions whether you agree or not. If you do disagree, then be candid when stating your position, but do so in a professional, non-threatening manner. Common ground is often found as a result of open, honest dialogue. Being open-minded to different opinions and ideas is the first step toward *acknowledging* the differences in others.

5. **Accept other people's contributions.** Consider others' contributions without demanding perfection. Control negativity by finding the positive aspects of others' inputs. Try not to immediately judge or stereotype, but take time to understand others' efforts. *Acceptance* is the first step toward *appreciating* the different contributions of others.

Because he had connected with many people in the organization, Jake was often asked for advice from his co-workers and peers. To help Gina develop relationships with her team members, Jake suggested she become more aware of other people at work besides her boss. He suggested that Gina should tune in to what her co-workers were doing and saying, so she could start building relationships with them.

Gina considered Jake's advice. She decided to arrive a few minutes early to the weekly team meeting. She took a seat in the back of the room instead of her normal seat at the table next to where the boss sat. As team members began to wander into the conference room, she casually mingled around the room, greeted everyone, and tried to join in their conversations. As the meeting began, she returned to her seat in the back of the room. She noticed those who sat around her were unusually quiet and reserved.

Later that day, as she stood in line at the cafeteria, she overheard a conversation occurring between two co-workers ahead of her.

"Hey, what's up with Gina trying to hang out with us at the meeting today?" Irene asked Frank.

"Yeah, I don't trust her. I think she's spying on us."

"Oh, I bet you're right. Why else would she try to talk to us and butt in our conversation?"

"Shhhh. Here she comes," Frank whispered as he turned to leave the room.

Gina was crushed when she heard this. After lunch, she hurried back to her office and called Jake, who explained a possible scenario.

"Don't you see, Gina? You've been so tight with the boss, it's only natural for people to be suspicious of you when you try to bond with them."

Jake suggested that Gina try talking with others who shared similar interests outside of work to help eliminate their distrust. She remembered she had heard Irene talking about her scrapbooking hobby. Gina had always wanted to learn how to scrapbook. She talked to Irene and began to build a relationship based on this common interest. Gina's connection with Irene began to grow and soon Gina and Irene began talking about mutual issues at work and working together to resolve them. Irene convinced the other members of the team that Gina was not a spy, enabling Gina to develop relationships within the team based on her awareness of others and her ability to earn their trust.

Jake knew that Frank needed help building relationships beyond the mentors he'd adopted. It had been another long, hard week at the office, and Jake was looking forward to his team's weekly gathering at the local pub on Friday afternoon. Meanwhile, Frank was looking forward to playing a round of golf with members of the senior staff that he had befriended; not only did he get to enjoy the time outdoors playing on his favorite course, but he got to hear the inside scoop on what was going on in the organization from his mentors.

"Any plans for the weekend, Frank?" Jake asked as he passed by Frank's office.

"Just the usual round of golf this afternoon, and I guess I'll watch the games on TV this weekend at home," Frank replied.

Later that day, Jake heard that the golf round had been cancelled. He stopped by Frank's office.

"Hey, Frank, what's up? You look kind of down." Frank explained his disappointment because of the cancellation of the weekly golf game. "Well, since you've got the afternoon free, why don't you come out with the gang? We're going to Happy Hour at O'Flanagan's," Jake offered. Frank hesitated, but eventually Jake talked him into going out with the team.

That afternoon at the pub, Frank was uncomfortable at first, but eventually loosened up and started talking to the others from work. As the afternoon turned into evening, Frank was having such a good time he didn't want to go home. He saw Jake and stopped to thank him. "I wouldn't have gotten to know everyone here if you hadn't convinced me into coming out. Thanks for helping me see what I'd been missing."

The following Monday, Jake reminded Frank that he should build on the success of Friday's social to open up more at work during interactions with his team members. Frank decided to share what his mentors had taught him with his team. When working with the team to put the finishing touches on a contract bid, Frank offered a suggestion.

"Why don't we run this by operations? They could give us a sanity check on whether this is a realistic proposal for our expected operating expenses," explained Frank.

"Are you kidding?" Gina shot back, "They're too busy."

"No, really," Frank said, "one thing the senior leaders taught me is that their most successful proposals have included review by operations." The team warmed up to Frank's suggestion, and warmed up to Frank as well. Once Frank became more approachable to others on his team, he began to connect with them in ways he never thought possible. He discovered that he could learn just as much from his peers as he had learned from his senior mentors.

As the "lone wolf" of the group, Elliott is distrustful due to being victimized by a co-worker in the past. Jake knew that in order for Elliott to build relationships, he had to learn how to trust again. He stopped by Elliott's office. As usual, the door was closed. Jake knocked and heard a gruff reply to come in.

"What do you want?" asked Elliott, impatiently.

"What are you working on?" asked Jake.

"None of your business!" shot back Elliott.

"OK, OK, I'm not here to get into your business so I can steal your ideas. I'm here to help," explained Jake. "Elliott, I know you are working on a proposal for our future products, and I'm not here to take that project away from you. I thought you might need some help and I have some information from an outside consultant that might be valuable input to your proposal."

Elliott stared back at Jake in disbelief. "I don't need your help," Elliott replied curtly. Jake put the consultant's report on Elliott's desk and left the office, hoping that Elliott would accept his help.

Elliott looked over the report Jake had left him, but still feeling like Jake had a hidden agenda for trying to help him, Elliott confronted Jake in his office. Jake suggested that Elliott needed to let go of the past wrongdoing by another co-worker and move on. It took lots of persuasion, but eventually Elliott realized he was consumed by anger about what happened. He admitted to Jake that he was tired of feeling that way and asked for his help with rebuilding his network.

Jake suggested that Elliott start by asking for help from others when needed. At the next team meeting, Elliott announced, "I am working on a proposal for the next generation of our product line. I can't do it alone. I need your help, so if you have any ideas, please let me know." The room was deathly silent. Elliott noticed everyone's jaws had dropped and people were staring at him in disbelief. Elliott was so embarrassed, he left the room. Jake spoke on Elliott's behalf.

"I know everyone is in shock, but Elliott really wants to forget the past and start being a part of this team. It was hard for him to speak up here today. I hope your reaction hasn't discouraged him."

Once the initial shock was gone, the members of the team left the meeting and stopped by Elliott's office, offering their help. Elliott was touched by everyone's outpouring of support and wished he had learned earlier to forgive and forget.

Irene found it difficult to acknowledge differences in opinions among her co-workers. Jake urged her to value these different opinions and helped her to reduce her tendency to avoid conflict. At the next team meeting, there were two choices facing the team on their release of the next product: release the product now, or postpone the product release until the marketing campaign was ready. There was significant disagreement on which decision was best and the team was split down the middle, with Irene conspicuously silent. Jake tried to make eye contact with her. Irene fought her natural tendency to remain neutral, but she had no desire to get tangled in the team's conflict. Jake gave her a gentle kick under the table, which spurred Irene to speak up.

"OK, look, I see both sides, but I'd like to give you my two cents, for what it's worth," Irene stammered.

"Go on," prompted Jake.

"Well, I see why we should go ahead and release the product now, but I don't think we should do anything without some input from marketing. Has anyone asked their opinion?" Irene steered the team toward a compromise, given input from the marketing department. She overcame her tendency to avoid injecting her opinion, and at the same time, helped her team be more open minded to the opinions of the marketing team. Although Irene was afraid at first to engage in debates or discussions, she began to forge deeper relationships with co-workers than she ever had when she remained neutral.

Jake noticed Haley's antagonistic attitude toward other work groups was based on her inclination to find fault in their efforts. With her blunt and competitive communication, her words often stung. He decided to try an experiment. He sent her an e-mail with a valid criticism of the performance of her team. Within five seconds of Jake hitting the "Send" button, Haley stormed into his office.

"How dare you take cheap shots at my team! This organization would be nothing without our team leading the way!" Jake stood up and tried to calm Haley down.

"Hold on a minute, I sent you that e-mail expecting the reaction you are having. Overall, your team performs well. Yes, I made a negative comment about your team. But I wanted you to know what your communication to others might feel like. How does it feel to receive that type of feedback?"

"How does it feel? It feels like you don't appreciate what my team is doing!"

Jake smiled and said, "Welcome to my world! That's how I've felt, along with all of the other team leaders, since you've been beating on our teams with your constant criticism."

Once Haley's anger had subsided and she realized that Jake's criticism wasn't meant to harm, Jake encouraged her to assess other teams' work more positively and pointed out how these groups supported her team. She realized she was taking the other groups' contributions for granted, and worked on breaking her negativity habit.

Sitting in the staff meeting with representatives from other teams, Haley found herself thinking how poorly the sales team was progressing toward meeting their monthly targets, but she bit her tongue. Rather than criticize sales, she realized how many new products her team had introduced and the extra responsibilities that had been placed on the sales team. She spoke up with a suggestion. "Sales is doing a good job but maybe they need some help. Has anyone thought about expanding our sales team?" Haley's suggestion prompted a discussion that resulted in approval to hire two more sales reps. Later, the sales team lead approached Haley.

"Wow, Haley, I really appreciate your idea to hire more sales reps. I thought you would be upset with our sales figures. I didn't expect that from you, of all people."

Haley replied with remorse, "No problem. I appreciate what you guys do and I'm sorry I wasn't more helpful earlier."

Ultimately, Jake helped Gina, Frank, Elliott, Irene, and Haley build rapport with others at work and to acknowledge, accept, and appreciate the differences in others. His co-workers began to realize the value of diversity, and discovered richer connections with the other people in their organization.

As you learn more about people, devote time to building new or renewed relationships, discuss views openly to reach deeper understanding, and respect what everyone brings to the table, you begin to reach a new level of connectivity with co-workers. While building deeper relationships, you begin to learn about others' strengths and weaknesses. Given this knowledge, you can build on those strengths, look for ways to improve the weaknesses, and utilize the contributions of all. As the collective, complementary strengths of the individuals working together are merged, the team or organization becomes more successful.

The Positive Force of Influence

Everyone is unique and original. When you truly value differences and can build on others' strengths to enhance your weaknesses, then you are equipped to effectively use the positive force of influence to achieve shared goals with your co-workers and peers. Exerting influence using a positive force results in a mutually beneficial outcome. The positive force of influence is inspiring and never manipulative or controlling.

In the midst of a major project, Jake saw his team falling apart. A battle of egos was ensuing, team members were at odds, and the team was being pulled in different directions. Although the team had built solid relationships based on their success with previous projects and their frequent socializing outside of work, they had major disagreements on how to proceed with their current project. The team's progress was at a standstill and Jake was at a loss as to how to get the team moving forward again, together.

At the next team meeting, Jake decided to use the positive force of influence to help build cooperation within his team. He called a time-out at the meeting as the recurring heated discussions began. He reminded everyone of the goals of the project, and asked for concurrence on these goals. Once he received public commitment from everyone, he emphasized the importance of these shared goals. He pointed out how everyone needed to apply their individual strengths to help each other to achieve these goals.

Next, Jake facilitated a brainstorming session to lay out the different approaches and plans for completing the project. Everyone on the team contributed their ideas and worked together to identify the pros and cons for each plan of action.

Finally, based on the collaborative effort to come up with options, the team began to discover the best way ahead through compromising to find the most efficient plan based on combining two of the options identified. The team agreed to this hybrid plan for their project and began to work together to carry out the plan.

Jake instinctively used his innate abilities to inspire and persuade his co-workers to cooperate, collaborate, and compromise. You can learn how to use these techniques to positively influence others to enable them to act and achieve shared goals. Here are the key skills you will need:

1. **Cooperate.** Cooperating requires helping others, not competing against them. Cooperation presumes there is no right or wrong, no better or worse. Part of cooperation is to help the other person understand what you want, and in turn, learn what the other person needs. Cooperating is an educational first step that lays the foundation for the next step, collaborating.

2. **Collaborate.** Collaborating requires working together to develop options and alternatives for reaching an agreement. Flexibility and creativity are essential for collaboration. Teaming up to discover possible solutions helps to set the stage for the next step, compromising.

3. **Compromise.** Compromising requires finding common ground based on the pool of possible solutions to the conflict. The desired outcome is a mutually beneficial, mutually satisfying resolution. There should not be any one-way concessions; each person should equitably give and take. If a solution that benefits both people cannot be found, then there should at least be agreement to disagree.

As Jake's team proceeded to execute the plan they had all agreed on, one of the team members, Irene, found herself growing uncomfortable with the schedule estimates they had developed for the tasks she was assigned. Irene had observed Jake during the last team meeting and admired him for his ability to positively influence the team. She decided to use Jake's approach to try to resolve her issues.

Irene approached Elliott to see if he could help her. "Hey, Elliott, I noticed you and I have some similar tasks for this big project, but it seems like I was given only three weeks to complete mine and you have five weeks," she explained. "There's no way I'm going to get my part done in that amount of time. Would you be willing to help me out?" she pleaded.

"No way, Irene! Do you realize how complicated my piece of this project is? That's why I was given two more weeks than you. And, besides, we all agreed on the schedule at the last meeting, so you're stuck," Elliott claimed adamantly.

Irene was stunned at Elliott's unwillingness to help. She couldn't believe Elliott thought his tasks were more difficult than hers, but decided not to react defensively. Instead, she conceded.

"OK, Elliott, I don't agree with your opinion of how difficult your tasks are compared to mine, but can you understand I need more time? And maybe you need someone to help you with your tasks?" She waited for Elliott to consider what she had said, hoping the conversation wouldn't escalate into a battle of wills, but thankfully he agreed with her assessment.

After Irene had gained Elliott's cooperation, she led him into a discussion of possible solutions to their problems. Elliott suggested they defer to Jake to help resolve the schedule issues, but Irene kept trying to convince Elliott that they could work it out on their own. After collaborating on possible solutions, and delving into the details of Elliott's tasks, Irene discovered that he'd been assigned a task she had some previous experience with, so she offered to help him.

"How are you going to have time to help me with that if you're already worried about getting your own work done on time?" Elliott asked.

"If I help you with this, then that would free up some of your time to help me finish my tasks in the first three weeks. We could work together during the last two weeks to finish up your part. Do you think that's doable?" Irene posed. Elliott was reluctant at first, but agreed with Irene's compromise.

Based on what she had learned from Jake, Irene was able to influence and persuade Elliott to resolve their schedule issues by demonstrating cooperation (helping Elliott to understand what she wanted, and in turn, learning what Elliott needed); collaborating to discover possible solutions; and compromising to reach a mutually satisfying resolution.

There is a significant added outcome each time the positive force of influence is used to reach compromises or inspire action. Not only are actions taken, results achieved, or decisions made to pave the way toward progress, but in the process of using the positive force of influence, relationships are strengthened. Connections with co-workers are reinforced based on the mutual trust that is bolstered during the process of cooperating, collaborating, and compromising, and in turn, the team or organization becomes more successful.

The Vibrancy of Co-worker Connections

As Elliott, Frank, Gina, Haley, Irene, and Jake have learned, connecting with co-workers starts with building vital relationships. By having empathy, finding common ground, and establishing mutual trust, relationships with peers and co-workers can be established; these relationships are more important than any other relationship in the work environment. Beyond building bonds with co-workers and peers, it is essential to acknowledge, accept, and appreciate the differences in others. By being aware of other people, learning to give and take, letting go of the past, keeping an open mind, and accepting other people's contributions, co-workers can value each others' inputs and learn the value of diversity. When co-workers truly value differences and can build on each others' strengths to enhance their weaknesses, they can effectively use the techniques of cooperation, collaboration, and compromising to inspire and influence each other to achieve shared success.

Valuing diversity and positively influencing others to achieve shared success are critical skills needed to have a successful career. While connecting with co-workers enhances you professionally and personally, just as important is the success of the organization. As co-workers connect, the team or organization becomes more productive, cohesive, and successful. In the end, everyone benefits in a robust and fulfilling way.

About
Deb Yeagle

Deb Yeagle found her passion in life as a personal coach, doing business as "Coach Deb." As a life and career coach, Deb helps others succeed in their personal and professional lives. Her coaching program includes an action-oriented approach to help clients achieve their goals and solve their problems. Through assessment, goal-setting activities, action planning, and moral support, Deb's personal coaching services ensure results in personal and professional development. Deb's goal with all her clients is to help them reach their full potential...to learn...to love...to laugh...and to *live*.

During the course of her coaching practice, Deb has published numerous articles on various topics including achieving life-work balance; curing workaholics; establishing effective time management habits; dealing with change; resolving conflict; avoiding communication breakdowns; and eliminating boring, monotonous routines.

Deb graduated from James Madison University (JMU) in Harrisonburg, Virginia, with a Bachelor of Science degree in Computer Science. She began her employment with the Federal Government in 1981 as a high school student apprentice, worked her way through college as a cooperative education student, and began a career in software and database development after graduation from JMU. She has over 13 years of experience in supervisory leadership, through which she gained practical experience in professional and personal coaching.

For more information, visit www.coachdeb.net. To contact Deb, call (540) 907-6789 or e-mail coachdeb@comcast.net.

Share the Guide to Getting It Series with Others

Call in your order for fast service and quantity discounts!
(503) 460-0014
OR Fax your order to 801-838-1671
OR order on-line at www.clarityofvision.com
OR order by mail: Make a copy of the order form below;
enclose payment information to:
Clarity of Vision, Inc.
3529 NE Simpson St.
Portland, OR 97211
Note: Shipping is $4.95 1st book + $1 for each additional book.

ORDER FORM: Send books to:
Name _____
Address _____
City _____ State ____ Zip _____
Phone: _____ Fax: _____ Cell: _____
E-Mail: _____
Payment by check or credit card
(VISA/MC/AMEX accepted.)
Name on card _____
Card Number _____
Exp. Date ____ Last 3-Digit number on back of card: ___

	Qty	Total Amount
Self-Esteem $14.95	____	_____
Achieving Abundance $14.95	____	_____
A Clear, Compelling Vision $14.95	____	_____
Remarkable Management Skills $14.95	____	_____
Powerful Leadership Skills $14.95	____	_____
Sacred Healing $14.95	____	_____
Purpose & Passion $14.95	____	_____
Creative Intelligence $14.95	____	_____
Vibrant & Lasting Relationships $14.95	____	_____
Branding & Marketing Mastery $14.95	____	_____